CASH FOR YOUR crafts

Wendy Rosen

Edited by Anne Childress   Design by Debi Wright

Distributed by Chilton Book Company

The Rosen Group, Inc.
3000 Chestnut Ave., Suite 300
Baltimore MD 21211
410.889.3093

First printing 1997
ISBN 0-8019-8917-5, pb
EAN 9 780801 989179
Written by Wendy Rosen

Editor: Anne Childress
Book Design: Debi Wright
Graphic Support: Bronté Roberts
Cover Design, Art Direction: Ashley Pound

about the author

LIKE THE THOUSANDS of craftspeople she serves, Wendy Rosen started her craft marketing business from a kitchen table when her children were still in diapers. The idea came to her on a visit to a craft show, where she discovered that the creativity artists displayed in their work wasn't always reflected in their use of business skills. At that moment, Wendy decided to leave a successful career in advertising to help artists learn how to market and sell their work.

Today her company, The Rosen Group, produces the Philadelphia Buyers Market of American Craft, which is the largest craft fair in the world with 1,500 exhibiting artists. In addition, Rosen publishes two large quarterly magazines: NICHE, a trade magazine for the owners of shops and galleries that carry American crafts; and AMERICANSTYLE, a consumer magazine for collectors and admirers of craft arts.

The Rosen Group helps to fill the marketing needs of more than 3,000 craft artists every year, including personal answers for those who write or call with business questions. It also maintains close relationships with thousands of craft shop and gallery owners who rely on the group's shows as their main source for craft work.

Every year Wendy speaks about crafts at universities, craft conferences and conventions. She has been featured on such television shows as "Working Woman" and QVC's "American Crafts with Phyllis George," and in such magazines as *Success, Family Circle, Redbook* and *McCall's*. Her first book, *Crafting as a Business*, has sold more than 50,000 copies since its publication in 1994.

The Rosen Group is headquartered in Baltimore's historic Mill Centre, a 19th-century textile factory that Wendy helped to restore and develop into a thriving arts center.

table of contents

acknowledgements

The ability to capture craft artists at work and the beauty of their handcrafted artwork is an art in itself. The photography used throughout this book was gratefully contributed by the following:

Bob Barrett
Ralph Gabriner
Eric Hanson
Glenwood Jackson
Bill Griffith
Leo Heppner
Vicki Kelch
Walter Larrimore
Robert Nicoll
George Post
Bill Schilling
Bob Stockfield
Norman Watkins
Steve Rosen

For the many hours spent verifying facts and sources on the telephone, thanks go to:

Mickie Workman
Jamie Weyandt

A very special thanks to the artists and crafts-people who are profiled in this book and to the artists whose creative handcrafted works are illustrated:

Bette Bell
Sandy Blaylock
Judie Bomberger
Julie Borodin
Susan Boss
Mark Brown
Mary-Ruth Chapin
Lucy Chittenden
Judy Crowell
Gabriel Cyr
Norah Curtis
Roberta Elias
Jill Elizabeth
Susan Feves
Betsy E. Fields
Kathlean Gahagan
Tzipora Hoynik
David and Dorothee Hutchinson
Liza Jarrett
Lynn Latimer
Margaret Lent
Sandra Magsamen
Thomas Mann
Robert Massa

Marsha McCarthy
Wendi Morris
Marissa Motto
Mary Lou Olszewski
Joy Owens
Ruth Ann Petree
Doug and Terri Phillips
Jan Richardson
Sheryl Schmidt
Duncan and Justin Schmidt
Erika Schmitt
Meredith Scott
Donna Lynne Shaw
Lucinda Shaw
Marion Shenton
Tracy Shue
Linda Shusterman
Jonathan Simons
Kim Dormandy Turner
Monika Turtle
Kim Weber
Marcie Zink
Denise Zukowski

Web pages:
Ferguson Taylor Group

introduction

WOULDN'T IT BE wonderful to make money doing the crafts you love? Could it be possible?

Twenty years ago the answer would have been a resounding NO. You couldn't dream anybody would buy something you created...you couldn't find a life in art...you certainly couldn't grow your hobby into something more.

Today things are very different. The craft community, once a loose group of individuals, is now a powerful movement with many resources for selling craftwork successfully.

The retail community has changed as well. A decade ago there were only a few hundred craft stores and galleries in the U.S. Now thousands of stores sell American crafts exclusively—and tens of thousands more include crafts as a specialty item on their shelves.

There's no better time to start a craft enterprise! The interest is lively and growing, and the demand for quality work is great. Best of all, it only takes a few hundred dollars and spare-time hours to make yourself a crafts entrepreneur, with a potential that reaches as high as your dreams can take you.

As you move into producing and selling your own crafts, please remember to keep in touch. We'd love to hear about your successes and help you with your problems.

Best of luck,

Wendy Rosen

You're an accomplished craftsperson with skills that have grown over the years and a flair for using your medium creatively. Now it's time to take the next step and begin to think about your craft in a new light: as a source of income.

1

new ways to think about crafts

why everybody loves crafts

HOW OFTEN do you find really wonderful and unusual things to buy? Shopping has become boring, with the same mass-market outlets everywhere you look. Mall owners have resorted to entertainment and celebrity appearances as a way of drawing customers. Even the nicest manufactured products are so widely advertised and discounted that they lose their specialness.

Crafts are individual, the product of a single hand and heart. In every handcrafted product the maker offers something very personal to each customer, and the customer cherishes the product. The individuality and personal expression of crafts are important to more and more customers tired of machine-made things.

People fall in love with handcrafts for other reasons, too. We want products that add value to our lives, support our relationships with others and feed our souls. We enjoy the feeling that we are participating in the maker's independent and creative lifestyle. We appreciate the chance to make beautiful, high-quality objects a part of our world.

The handwork you do will appeal to customers who feel this way. They are already receptive to the idea of buying crafts. All you need to do is prepare yourself and your work to meet their expectations.

a new level of skill

CHANCES ARE you began doing crafts with kits, patterns and hobby supplies. Now you need to set yourself apart from the hobby crowd. The success of a craft enterprise will depend on your creative ability to make items that are very different from the basic projects sold in stores. After all, they only involve hand finishing of machine-made components, with the resulting piece identical to every other piece produced with the same kit. It's a useful way to learn craft skills, but it's not craft art.

You will need some new skills to make highly saleable and unique crafts based on your own ideas and designs. The following table gives some common skills and some complementary new skills that will expand your ability to make distinctive, beautiful crafts. You'll find classes at your local high school, college, arts center or arts guild. If you have the time and money, schedule a course at one of the major craft or art schools

Category	New Skill
Sewing	Dyeing Woodblock printing Silkscreening Silk painting Batik and wax resist Millinery
Molded ceramics & polymer clay	Lampworking with glass Wheel or slab ceramics
Woodworking	Lathe turning Faux painting
Bead stringing & jewelry assembly	Metalsmithing Jewelry making Soldering Metal stamping Lost wax casting

with classes designed specifically for adults seeking technical skills in crafts; they're listed in the Resources chapter at the end of this book.

creativity & production

TO GO ALONG with your new skills, you'll need a new way to think about the crafts you do. The best path to successful sales is through "production crafts"—that is, craft pieces that are made by the dozens or hundreds (sometimes thousands!) from a single design created by the artist. Production crafts are sold at fairs and through fine gift stores and craft galleries...even at Tiffany's!

When you do production crafts, your talent comes into play at three points:

- In designing the original piece.
- In modifying the original so that each piece can be finished in a reasonable time.
- In creating the pieces themselves.

That's not the same as spending hours and hours of loving attention on each project, but craft artists find it just as satisfying. For many of them, it means a profitable sideline that gives the family all those "extras" everyone wants. For others, it expands into a full-time business that offers a world of new opportunities.

The rest of this book will show you how to put your new thinking about crafts to work. In the next chapter you'll find specific information about 10 exciting and imaginative craft enterprises that people like you have started successfully, plus profiles of artists.

Subsequent chapters have practical ideas that can benefit all types of craft enterprises. The last chapter is a comprehensive list of resources to help you.

The great majority of today's successful craft artists started out on a small, part-time basis...just as you will. Here are 10 ideas for the kinds of craft enterprises that can set you on your road to success, plus profiles of established artists who once took the same road themselves.

2

10 great ideas

surface design & decorative pai

THERE IS no greater satisfaction than taking something old and worn and recycling it into something new and beautiful. There is good profit, too! Some of the most popular items to paint include wooden boxes and baskets, furniture, plant stands, toys and clothing. You might also add old scraps such as knobs, buttons and trim to your pieces for an unusual look.

Of course, you don't have to limit yourself to old pieces. You can make all kinds of new accessories: napkin rings, mailboxes, floorcloths, placemats, tiles, boxes and more. There are wonderful opportunities for customizing your work, too, by adding a name or date that's special to the buyer.

> ## Start-up Costs
> Under $150
> ## Start-up Supplies
> Unfinished pieces, paint, business cards, samples
> ## Skills
> Drawing, lettering, faux painting, "antiquing," decoupage and stenciling

Popular trends include designs that use primitive American art, art deco, Caribbean or ecological themes. Sayings and poems add special value. Don't worry about being too colorful. It doesn't matter whether your piece will "go" with other furniture in the room—you're making art! Where to sell? Home shows will give you the chance to display your talents in your own booth or in demonstration workshops.

Wholesale craft shows, gift shows or clothing shows can be good sales venues, too, depending on the kind of pieces you produce. An exciting possibility is charity "showcase" houses, where you could work with interior designers to create unique pieces that sell for up to $1,000.

artist's profile: sandra magsamen

Sandra Magsamen has loved art and crafts for as long as she can remember. Her first career was as an art therapist, working with the elderly.

The birth of her daughter Hannah crystallized Sandra's desire to work from home. Craft art was the natural choice; as Sandra says, "Expressing myself in words has never been natural, but painting and drawing always gave me an outlet." She has developed a line of tiles, bowls, placemats,

floorcloths and more that are sold in small shops and major department stores across the country. Many of the pieces include the words she finds so hard to say, with romantic imagery and messages that lift the spirit. How does she develop new ideas and images? "As I learn things in my life, I incorporate them into my work. My tiles and other pieces are decorated with sayings that strike a chord with me, and a lot of them teach lessons I think people need to remember."

Today, the Magsamen home is filled with art made by Sandra, husband Mark (a gifted painter) and dozens of artist friends. "Surrounding yourself with beautiful objects and appreciating the beauty around you makes life richer," she says.

interior design

WITH A lot of good taste and a very little bit of start-up money, you can go far as an interior designer. Although most designers and decorators concentrate on home design, there are good opportunities in corporate offices, hospitals, religious institutions, country clubs, small hotels (especially bed and breakfasts)—even cruise ships!

> ### Start-up Costs
> Under $200
> ### Start-up Supplies
> Business cards, photo portfolio of work
> ### Skills
> Design skill, basic knowledge of architecture and materials, awareness of building codes and other laws

Selling your design abilities is a tough job when you don't have much of a track record. It's often best to donate your services for the first few projects to get off to a running start. Here are other ideas for getting your talents in front of the public:

- Design a small corner or room vignette for retail shops, with the agreement that your business cards and a sign be prominently displayed. Be sure to give the retailer a finder's fee or gift for client referrals.
- Volunteer as a guest speaker at professional and women's organizations.
- Offer two hours of consulting time to be raffled at an elegant benefit event.
- Set up a room vignette at home or garden shows.
- Team up with a real estate developer or builder to decorate a model home or apartment.
- Ask fabric stores to refer clients to you. Offer some incentive to each salesperson. Ask if you can make a presentation to the sales staff before the store opens. Ask to be part of the store's special events.
- Find a small newspaper or magazine that will allow you to write a regular column of decorating trends and tips—including a special note that indicates you are a local designer.

artist's profile: joy owens

When she moved back to her hometown (Baltimore) in 1986, Joy Owens considered opening a store. She'd once had a wicker business, selling furniture and accessories and doing the occasional basketry wall arrangement for a customer. Now she wanted to expand the design service component.

To prepare, she studied interior design at a local community college—and became so interested that the store was put on hold in favor of Joy Owens Interiors, founded in 1992.

"My first office was the kitchen table," she says. "When my books had taken over the kitchen, I moved my husband out of his den. Then I took over the garage and the basement." Today she has an office in the city's central business district and two employees.

Ninety percent of Joy's business comes from

stores and other commercial businesses. Recent projects include designing a museum exhibit in Philadelphia, working with an architectural firm to create luxury suites and lobbies for the new Baltimore Ravens football stadium, and designing public spaces and model apartments for low-income elderly housing.

"I think of myself as an urban interior designer," she says. "Many of my projects involve revitalizing the inner city. I've gone into areas no one else has—like low-income housing, where my designs are geared to the financial level of the users. I believe in giving people a chance who ordinarily wouldn't get it."

Joy has three grown children and four grandchildren. "Older women don't realize you can make a living from creative work," she says. "We're all living longer. We can have several careers. Women can prepare for something new as they retire."

event planning & decorating

THE TRADITIONAL entry into this field is floral design. Customers want to add drama to weddings and special events with flowers to swag across windows and fireplaces...wind down staircases...trail across elegant banquet tables. The look combines the beauty of flowers with the casual touch of vines, leaves and grasses. It's far beyond the "arrangements" that most florists rely on.

Your success will depend on providing services that standard storefront florists don't: imagination, creativity, willingness to spend time with each client. Your client list will grow through networking with business professionals and people with gracious homes—busy people with little time and a need for your higher level of service.

From floral design it's an easy step to planning and decorating the entire event. It's best to start with small events for existing clients, both individuals and companies. You can stage a New Year's Eve party for a two-career couple, an employee picnic for a business or a volunteer recognition dinner for a hospital. Some event planners specialize in one area, such as weddings or business conventions. Others are known for creating theme parties around local landmarks.

Even small businesses will spend as much as $10,000 on a party.

So will private clients. Because you buy in bulk, you can get lower prices on food, decorations, entertainment, labor and supplies. A good source of profit lies in renting out your handcrafted decorations over and over again. Some of your profit will come from marking up these costs, the rest from using your own creative energy to make something exciting from standard supplies.

Your new best friend will be the closest wholesale florist. These suppliers carry an incredible array of fresh and dried flowers, along with a generous selection of containers, ribbons and "props." You'll also learn who can be relied on in hotel catering and convention departments, other caterers, musicians, photographers, display companies and theater supply companies.

artist's profile: mary-ruth chapin

As a child, Mary-Ruth Chapin followed her grandmother through the family garden, soaking up the secrets of keeping cut flowers alive, drying vines and creating arrangements with old-fashioned charm. Working for the telephone company

in Washington, D.C., she supervised the installation of phones for hotel conferences and conventions. Each time she entered a luxurious hotel lobby, she was drawn to the elaborate floral displays and holiday decorations. And, as she had years before in her grandmother's garden, she stored up ideas.

When husband Peter started his own company in 1986, Mary-Ruth decorated his offices. Her business grew out of favorable comments on that one job—and today she's the local Martha Stewart! Her work has expanded from flower arrangement and interior design to include wedding planning, which now makes up half the business. Her customers are often busy professional women looking for an experienced creative person to guide them through one of life's most complicated events.

"I do things other florists just can't do, like gathering wild vines and flowers," Mary-Ruth says. "My arrangements are more loose, casual and unusual than the FTD look. What florist would stand by the bride and pin each corsage and boutonniere on the bridesmaids and groomsmen?

"The result is that the wedding party can be guests at their own event, instead of worrying about a thousand details."

clothing design

YOU ARE an excellent seamstress, but you'll need some real art skills to make a living in clothing and costume design. You'll also need the imagination and flair to create clothes that customers won't find elsewhere.

Start-up Costs
$200

Start-up Supplies
Sewing materials and equipment, business cards, portfolio

Skills
Quilting, appliqué, dyeing, painting, stenciling, silk screening, weaving, felting, beading, pattern-making, fitting

Manufacturers of ready-to-wear clothes design and produce new items five times a year (fall, winter, resort, spring and summer). You'll be better off concentrating on a very narrow market where you can become an expert quickly.

One of the fastest growing market segments is original Halloween costumes for children and adults (who are taking over what used to be "kids' night out"). Or you could create T-shirt designs based on local landmarks...embellish ready-to-wear goods...make hats, purses and other accessories...specialize in children's clothes. In addition to people who go to craft fairs, your customers could be dance schools, local theater groups, musical groups, costume rental shops, even party planners.

Small craft fairs are a good way to start. Presenting your work at a boutique as a trunk show event is another great option. Later, you can move on to major retail and wholesale shows.

artist's profile: monika turtle

Monika Turtle wanted to sew from the time she was 7 or 8 years old—and the way she fashioned a career from her skills could serve as a pattern for your own success.

First came school, then an apprenticeship with a costume company in Philadelphia, then a decision to make just one product: velvet hats. "I tried selling six hats at a flea market," Monika says. "It opened at 10 a.m., and I sold out by 10:15. The next week I made 12 hats, and they were gone by noon. After six weeks or so, I realized I was doing what people really wanted.

"I think flea markets and small craft fairs are a great way to begin. The fee for the table is only $20 or $25, and you get a feel for what people want to buy. Check out the markets first; look for the ones that are open every week with good products, customers and variety. Even if you don't find what you want right away, it's just a nice thing to do on a Saturday afternoon."

Her next step was to approach a Philadelphia gallery that sold beginning artists' work on consignment. Monika began with a dozen, which sold out in two weeks and earned her a place on the gallery's list of regular suppliers. "Our future lies in selling to stores, not directly to customers," she says. "You can't do retail shows in areas where stores sell your work, and we now have about 350 stores nationally."

Monika's clothing line has expanded to include reversible long and short velvet coats, suits, pants, skirts, jackets, purses and muffs. She produces spring/summer and fall/winter collections each year, and works with many different fabrics and colors. "Actually," she says, "I started with black velvet exclusively because I could only afford to buy one fabric in one color, and it became a kind of signature. Even now, the line is always based on black."

She adds, "When I started I knew very little about where to sell crafts. You should never be afraid to ask, though. Craft people are very open and generous with information."

jewelry making

TWENTY YEARS ago, most jewelry was made in factories and foreign sweatshops. Today, customers look for unique fashion jewelry made by American designers.

This recent major development sets the seal on the trend toward individualism: Wholesale distributors of jewelry supplies are opening their doors to small home-based businesses! You can

Start-up Costs
$200 and up
Start-up Supplies
Vary with the type of jewelry
Skills
Design, beading, metalworking, gemsetting, fabric arts, ceramics, painting, braiding, knotting, enameling

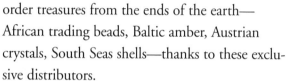

order treasures from the ends of the earth— African trading beads, Baltic amber, Austrian crystals, South Seas shells—thanks to these exclusive distributors.

Jewelry can be as simple as stringing beads, as difficult as diamond-cutting. Some of the most appealing designer pieces evoke natural forms like flowers, leaves and snowflakes; others are based on an area's culture (for example, Southwestern patterns). Customers like to buy pieces that express their interests or their religious beliefs as well.

It's often preferable to sell jewelry through shops. When a store or gallery sells your work they really earn their profit, and you gain more time to do the work you love. A shop will double ("keystone") the cost of each piece you sell them. The wholesale price of your jewelry is half the retail price you put on your work at a retail fair.

artist's profile: jill elizabeth

"The key is to develop a style of your own," says Jill Elizabeth. "Imitative styles are okay—they're part of growing—but you need to dig deeper to find your own voice. That's when you become an artist."

Jill didn't find her voice until she'd spent years working as a jeweler, for others and then for herself. Or, as she puts it, "The chrome found me."

The chrome is an aluminum polyethylene laminate with a mirrored surface, most often used in places like hotel lobbies. Jill had picked up a sample at a display industry trade show. For weeks it lay on her workbench in a scatter of colored wire and beads...calling to her, insisting it had the image she was looking for.

And so it did: a figure who stepped from an Egyptian frieze, a light-bearer holding a crystal who has become Jill's personal muse. That was the first of several hundred vivid and decorative pieces in the successful Liztech line, all of them hand-cut from mirrored chrome and hand-decorated with beads, crystals, shells, wire and floss. Their gleaming, jeweled images dance out of an imaginary world: goddesses and sprites, firebirds and mermaids, wizards and dragons, kachina and yei and a dozen other figures from Southwestern legends.

Jill credits her early years with other jewelers for some of the success: "I not only learned many styles of production and ways to do art, I learned business practices—all the things they never teach you in school. I could pick the best of many people."

Her early years in small craft fairs helped, too. "I learned that selling is engaging people and making them comfortable. People who go to craft shows are interested in you as well as your art. They want to be in touch with the independent lifestyle.

"Your customers are the reason you do your work. Treat them like royalty!"

garden accessories

GARDEN accessories have become a real growth industry since the early 1990s, when baby boomers began to buy larger homes. As with everything else they do, the boomers are putting their own stamp on gardens by inventing all kinds of new accessories.

Fortunately, a lot of the new and newly popular items are ideal for the beginning craft artist. Think of garden stakes in the shape and color of

Start-up Costs
$100-$500

Start-up Supplies
Business cards and portfolio, plus materials and equipment for the type of craft you make

Skills
Woodworking, metal crafting, appliqué

each vegetable in the patch...plaques with poems and sayings...wind chimes...whirligigs...flags and banners.

If you're a woodworker, there's a wide choice of more traditional items: bird feeders, mailboxes, planters and benches, to name a few. For sculptors, sculpture and bird baths are possibilities. One popular garden sculptor began with empty steel tanks from the junkyard!

Ask local florists and garden shops to carry your work. Become a speaker at garden club meetings. Exhibit at home, flower and garden shows, which draw the people who are most likely to buy from you.

Some of the country's biggest flower shows are held every year in New York City, Philadelphia and Washington, D.C. They're excellent sources of ideas—as well as goals to set for your own displays some day.

artist's profile: marion shenton

Marion Shenton's skills are sewing, quilting and design, and she combined them a decade ago to help pay for college by making windsocks and selling them as a street vendor in Philadelphia. She also worked part-time with a professional quiltmaker, who allowed her to make some of her own designs.

After college she started her own company, with windsocks as her first product line. "They sold well," she says. "I added wall hangings next,

based on some pieces I did for my family. Then I began making flags, too, because my customers kept asking for them." The customers were looking for something better than mass-produced

flags, and Marion responded with bright abstract designs in fade-resistant nylon.

"The wind banners are doing really well," she says. "You can put them directly in the ground or hang them like regular flags. I plan to do larger and more intricate ones in the future, and I'm also starting to think about room screens."

Marion began by marketing at retail craft fairs, but for the past six years she has used wholesale markets and trade magazine advertising exclusively. She also designs custom-made flags on commission. Her company, Wind's Edge, sends most of its sewing work out to cottage crafters who work from their homes.

"I think it's important to offer a range of styles, sizes and prices, even at the beginning," Marion says. "I remember we did a 12-foot windsock as an eyecatcher for our display booth, and it sold our six-foot socks for us. Now that 12-foot sock sells, too!

"I also think beginning craft artists should make sure they're doing something they enjoy a lot, because they'll be spending lots of long hours. And you can't be easily discouraged. There will be disappointments, but you can learn from them."

religious objects

P EOPLE have always made beautiful art as an expression of their faith. Crafts are perfect for religious objects, because they are expressive in a way that is very personal—to the maker and the buyer alike. Almost every type of craft lends itself to religious works.

Start-up Costs
$100-$500

Start-up Supplies
Business cards and portfolio, plus materials and equipment for the type of craft you make

Skills
Vary according to the type of craft

Stained glass panels, home altars, picture frames, statuettes, crosses, Nativity creches, Christmas tree ornaments and stars, jewelry using Christian emblems and symbols are appropriate Christian possibilities.

Jewish themes include menorahs (Sabbath seven-branch or Hanukkah nine-branch), mezuzahs, dreidels, Stars of David, havdalah sets, Seder plates, challah covers, matzoh covers, embroidered talliths and yarmulkes and kiddush cups.

While not based on a specific religion, the celebration of Kwanzaa evokes such deep feelings that it belongs here, too. The beautiful sculpture, fabrics and jewelry of Africa can inspire endless craft ideas, especially for works that express the attributes Kwanzaa stands for.

artist's profile: lucinda shaw

"It started as a challenge," says Lucinda Shaw, who was teaching nursery school when a colleague brought in some bits of glass intended for a suncatcher. "The colors were good and the idea attracted me. I decided to see if I could make something, too." Lucinda had always painted. Now the idea of creating with glass took hold. She took courses in working with lead and copper foil, painting in glass, enameling, carved and etched glass and fused glass. Her pieces—always from her own designs—grew larger.

Still, she didn't think of her art as a career. She worked at a tack shop, then managed a vineyard. "I knew it was in my blood," she says, "but I only realized it was my life's work after I divorced and went back to college." She spent her junior year in England (including an apprenticeship), went back after graduation and began accepting commissions.

Today she has her own studio in Baltimore, where she works from commissions and teaches glass art. Her pieces are largely religious and go beyond stained glass windows; she was commissioned to create a carved glass view of Baltimore's Basilica of the National Shrine of the Assumption of the Blessed Virgin Mary, which was presented to Pope John Paul II when he visited the city. Work comes to her through word of mouth and advertisements in glass arts and religious magazines.

"I do a lot of meditation," Lucinda says. "Sometimes I wake up in the morning with a completed window. I firmly believe we are guided by a higher power. I'm told my work has a healing influence, and I would hope that is true. Certainly it always has a healing element."

31

ceramic accessories

THE NICE thing about ceramic accessories is that they can often be made in a limited work space and fired in a small kiln. Thrown work is probably the hardest technique to master. Slip-cast work is easier but requires space for large molds (and you should make your own molds if you want pieces that are truly distinctive). Slab work is easiest of all—like cutting a dress pattern or making cookies!

What to make? Door number plates, accent tiles, name plates, clocks, picture frames, jewelry, Christmas tree ornaments, stand-alone pieces (flowers, little houses, animals, etc.). Theme possibilities are endless. How about a picture frame for a fisherman who wants to prove he caught The Big One? Tiles in quilt designs? A plaque for a baby's room? Garden stakes? This is a craft where your imagination can really take flight!

> **Start-up Costs**
> $100-$500
>
> **Start-up Supplies**
> Molds, wheel, clay, paint, glaze, kiln; business cards and samples
>
> **Skills**
> Slip-cast, slab and thrown techniques

artist's profile: jan richardson

"At first it was just me working on the kitchen table," says Jan Richardson, who cut the first slab for a pottery house in 1977. "This was long before houses became the rage. I made them because I liked them as a kid."

Jan's equipment was minimal; she even worked as studio manager at the local junior college in exchange for use of its kiln. Her work was always highly detailed and time-consuming, with as many as several hundred pieces that had to be cut and attached individually. "I realized very soon that I would need people to help," she says. "I mean, I couldn't ask my kids to put shingles on houses forever." Windy Meadows Pottery—

named after the farm near Harpers Ferry, W.Va., where Jan and her family live—grew rapidly. It invaded the farmhouse basement and the tractor shed, took over a gallery in the house itself, found office space in the hayloft, and eventually added mobile units for production.

"I think one reason for our growth is that I had prior retail experience: a dress shop when the kids were little," Jan says. "I understand where retailers are coming from, and I really like the business and marketing part."

One major decision was to develop a line of houses in three different sizes and price ranges. Another was to offer numbered limited editions with a certificate of authenticity for each piece. As for marketing: "I think it's a real advantage to advertise to your own mailing list, although we also take some ads in collectibles or country life magazines. And, of course, we do wholesale shows.

"The basis for success is having your own vision that you feel you must bring into being. But it's very important to have a business plan, too."

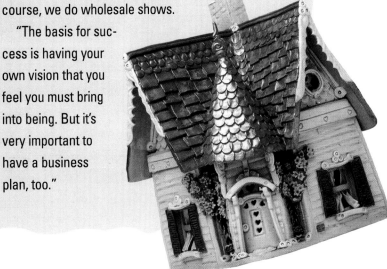

children's goods

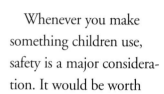

LIKE CERAMIC accessories, children's goods cover a range of craft arts. If you work with fabric, you could make clothing, toys, wall hangings, quilts or blankets. Ceramic possibilities include cups and dishes, plaques, night lights and picture frames. Woodworkers can make toys and furniture; painters can decorate what the woodworkers and clothing designers make. There's a growing market for children's jewelry, too.

Start-up Costs
$100-$500

Start-up Supplies
Business cards and portfolio, plus materials and equipment for the type of craft you plan to make

Skills
The type of items you make will determine the skills

Whenever you make something children use, safety is a major consideration. It would be worth your time to check local, state and federal laws and product regulations.

Demographers tell us there's a baby boomlet underway. Take advantage of it!

artist's profile: sheryl schmidt

Like many craft artists, Sheryl Schmidt had another career in mind when she started out. Her degree in graphic design and advertising art prepared her well for jobs with a marketing firm, printer, design studio and several advertising agencies—it's just that she didn't like the work much.

"It wasn't nearly as interesting as I thought it would be, and not much of a creative outlet, either," she says. "Plus, it's very demanding of your time. If I'm going to work those hours I want it to be for myself."

She quit when she became pregnant with her second child in 1994, and found the creative outlet she wanted in painting. With her mind on children and a desire to have her own business, she settled on painting nursery furniture.

"I learned the techniques in courses, and I saw the right way to use them in a job I had once." Themes can come from nursery rhymes, classic children's books, Bible stories or Sheryl's own imagination. "I don't know why, but there have been a lot of bunnies lately," she says. "And leaves are starting to appear everywhere in my work." In addition to furniture, which she buys unfinished from a craft cooperative, her product lines include wall hangings ("they're like removable murals for the nursery") and floorcloths. And though she is relatively new to craft arts, custom orders are already starting to come in.

"I'm convinced that superior quality and an individual touch will bring buyers," Sheryl says. "I also believe in listening to the customer and working within his or her budget."

For now, Sheryl's studio is in her home, a roomy Victorian in a historic district. For others with home offices, she has a final piece of advice: "Establish a starting time and a cutoff time for work. When you're through for the day, physically get out of the house for a bit. Take a walk. Give the dog a run. Separate the two parts of your life and you'll be much happier."

paper arts & paper making

PAPER ARTS are great for launching a home-based business.

Minimal equipment and low-cost supplies are two of the best reasons. A third is the high demand for customized and personalized cards and stationery. Better shops are selling original greeting cards for as much as $20 apiece, which means your wholesale price can be as much as $10.

Say a word of thanks to Hallmark for persuading Americans to send cards on every occasion. Your own work will find a niche among people who want something that goes well beyond the mass-produced—and are willing to

> ### Start-up Costs
> $100 and up
> ### Start-up Supplies
> Paper, fabric, beads, metals, other production materials; business cards and samples
> ### Skills
> Design, calligraphy, assemblage, paper cutting and paper making

pay for it. You stand a good chance of picking up custom work, too, as people see your work and want you to create something for a special occasion in their own lives. Wouldn't it be fun to design a card proposing marriage, complete with engagement ring?

Not all artists who work in paper do cards and stationery, of course. They may make the paper itself, or use other artists' handcrafted papers in book covers, photo albums, collages, accessories like picture frames and lampshades, as well as jewelry. Papier-maché lends itself to sturdier objects, even furniture.

artist's profile: wendi morris

A self-taught artist and calligrapher with a sure sense of design, Wendi Morris has been making her vivid and cheerful cards for three years. She moved to cards after specializing in custom gift wrapping, originally a hobby she did for friends.

"The card business is certainly more lucrative

than gift wrapping was," she says, "but that's not why I changed over. It's because this is something I just love to do. It's a tremendous creative outlet."

Wendi's cards layer handmade papers on a good white stock, then add fabrics, beads, charms, "anything and everything that's different." Curlicues of paper and ribbon have become a signature touch. "Ideas just come to me," she says. "Or I may see something. I saw some really pretty baby booties once, and they wound up on one of my most successful cards."

Wendi doesn't keep an inventory. Instead, she presents customers with a variety of designs (more than 200 created so far) and works from their orders. Most customers are stationery stores. She sends samples and offers to pay return postage if the retailer doesn't like them. In three years, only one package has come back.

She has also tried selling through the Philadelphia Buyers Market of American Craft. "It's a completely different group," she says. "To stationery people, what I do is just another card. To crafters, it's art. Naturally, I enjoy that kind of feedback!"

As colorful and effervescent as her cards are, Wendi says that "my life is plain beige—my clothes, my home, everything. I guess I put everything into my craft."

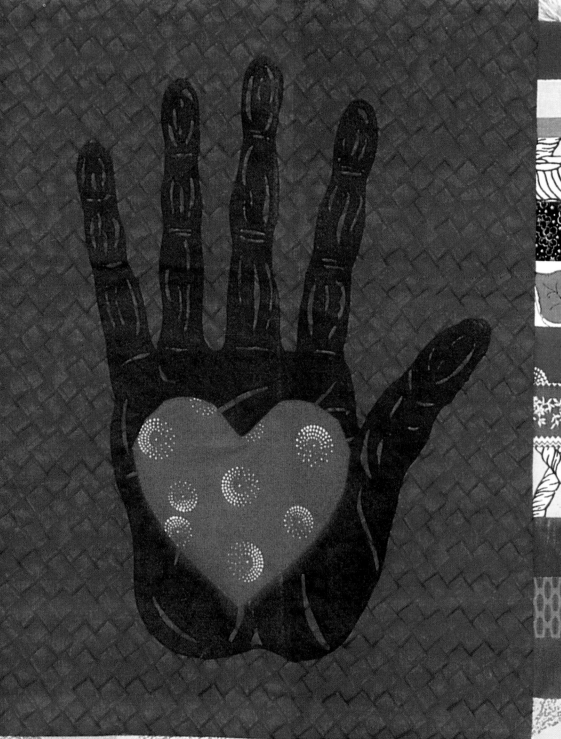

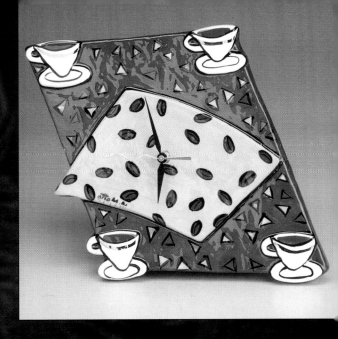

Becoming a craft artist with a unique product line means taking a good look at how this new undertaking will affect your life. Here are some thoughts that will help you make a smooth transition.

3

great start-up strategies

your special needs

Space

The traditional place for start-ups is the garage, but a spare bedroom, attic or basement will work just as well. The key is to keep the beads and baskets and bits of clay off the kitchen table and out of the family's living space.

You will need storage shelving or cabinets, enough table space for your work and an area for a mini-office—desk, phone, answering machine, fax, typewriter or computer. Estimate that you will keep about one month's finished production on hand. You will also need space for an additional month's production in progress.

If you depend on custom-designed work, you will need someplace to meet customers. Are you comfortable using your home for this? Alternatives are a store, art center, gallery, classroom or interior decorator's office.

Money

All crafts require an initial investment. In the last chapter we supplied some rough estimates for start-up costs, but your situation could easily be different. Do you need to buy office equipment? Office supplies? Stationery? Furniture? Add those costs to the amounts you will spend on craft supplies. Then ask the big question: Can I afford to spend that? Can I afford it even if I never earn a dime? Worst-case scenarios are useful, even if improbable.

Since you will be earning money, you definitely need to talk to a tax expert. The rules covering home-based businesses are complicated, and you should not try to deduct office space, supplies, etc., without the help of someone who knows the way through the maze.

Time

One of the best reasons for going into production crafts is time flexibility. When you work for yourself you can often arrange your work schedule to meet personal needs and family obligations. Customers may still call you on the phone at all hours, but an answering machine will help you keep your life manageable.

You will probably find that some seasons or months are busier than others. If you make Christmas items, for example, August through November will be your busy time. Develop a line that will sell throughout the year if you want to avoid seasonal ups and downs.

Time, Money & Efficiency

Production efficiency is the key to profit. Break down the steps of the production cycle so that you can work on several items at once.

Buy supplies in quantities that are realistic but large enough to give you a full discount and keep you from running short. Estimate how many items you can make in a day, week and month.

Analyze your time and energy carefully. Start with a simple calendar, and commit to making a certain number of items each week. You can also commit to a specific dollar amount of production value.

Find a block of time when you can concentrate on work. Many craftspeople begin work after dinner or after the children are in bed. Early risers get up before dawn. If you work without distraction, your efficiency improves.

what will you make?

CRAFTS ARE produced in a special way...but also for special people. To succeed, it's important to understand how the marketplace for this type of merchandise works.

Big manufacturers design products that will sell to the mass market. Success is measured in the number of mass-produced items they sell. On the other hand, most craft studios concentrate on specialty items that appeal to a much smaller group of people.

Successful craft artists seek customers who belong to a special interest group or lifestyle, or who are part of a trend. (Fads that have already hit the mass market are too late for you, unless your product is unusual or of higher value and quality.)

Luckily, no matter how narrow the interest group, you will probably be able to contact these potential customers through specialty magazines, databases, referrals, mailing lists, special events, conventions and more. The best places to start are the library and the Internet. Publications for specific groups can be found in *Bacon's Publicity Checker* or *Standard Rate and Data*. The American Society of Association Executives in Washington, D.C., can help you find special-interest organizations.

Tomorrow's Trends

What special interests should be your market? Where are the next big trends? Chances are they're right in front of you. Here are the places to look.

Museum exhibitions

Did you know that each year more people pay to attend art events than sports events? Blockbuster art exhibitions have a nationwide (sometimes worldwide) impact. Look back at some of the memorable exhibitions of the last 20 years—Tutankhamen, ancient China, Monet, Andrew Wyeth—and remember the tidal wave of products that followed.

Movies, music & television

Every season new shows and stars create cult groups, and old ones pick up new followers. Our kids are putting up posters of James Dean!

Examples: the Beatles, the Grateful Dead, Star Trek (which still hasn't peaked after 30 years) and classic movies with the Marx Brothers, Marilyn Monroe and Humphrey Bogart.

Sports

Team insignia can only be reproduced by companies willing to pay a stiff licensing fee. It's best to look for sports categories that are small, growing and have participants that are affluent and in their 40s. Examples: scuba diving, hot air ballooning, tennis, yoga, golf, bicycle touring.

Social action

So many of us have little time to help others. Buying products that have messages of support or that include a donation with the purchase make us feel we can be part of the solution. Examples: the environment, the homeless, children at risk, historic preservation.

Belief systems & practices

Art has always been connected to belief, from ancient statues of the gods to modern stained-glass installations in churches and synagogues everywhere. Judaica items like menorahs, Seder plates and dreidels are becoming popular additions to holiday celebrations for Christians as

well—a way of honoring the foundations of Christian beliefs and expressing tolerance and support for others' celebrations. In addition, African-Americans' interest in their heritage has made the observance of Kwanzaa increasingly important. For all of us, beliefs give meaning to our lives and connect us with our past.

Art & culture

Inspiration can come from every civilization and era: African, Native American, Renaissance, ancient Egyptian, Asian, Colonial, Byzantine.

Education

Any subject—earth science, biology, chemistry, political science, history—can inspire an interesting product. Examples: genealogy charts, molecular design prints.

Anti-fad

Sometimes the best path to a new product is in the other direction. Every really popular trend can lead you to a great new idea. Remember the "Baby on Board" car window signs that spawned all kinds of imitations? Think about anti-golf products for golf widows, anti-cooking products for professional women and so on.

Problem-solvers

Crafts in this category give customers special benefit in addition to beauty and quality. Just be sure you provide a clear message (perhaps a hang tag or certificate) about the intended use. Examples: remote control keepers, magnets for the dishwasher that say "Clean" or "Dirty," message center for the refrigerator, special place for car keys, anything with a message that serves as a reminder (clean your room, walk the dog, etc.).

Fashion

Next year's home decor colors and fabrics are often on the fashion show runways or the pages of *Vogue* right now.

Regional differences

Trends in America tend to start in big cities

and coastal ports, where imports from abroad reach us, then move toward the center of the country. New York and Los Angeles are always great places to look for trends.

Design

Choose a popular design vocabulary that suits your own style. Examples: Art Deco, Art Nouveau, Victorian, country and folk art.

History

Almost every period has its devotees. Here in America, interest is strong in our own rich past: Native American culture, Victoriana, the '20s, the '60s. And fascination with the Civil War seems to grow stronger every year.

Don't forget local history and culture. Pennsylvania Dutch stencils, Mardi Gras masks, the picturesque life of the Old West and the Gold Rush days—the lore of your own area can be the best source of inspiration.

Nature

Love of nature and commitment to conservation are among the strongest currents in American life today. Evoke these feelings through your crafts— especially if you take your themes from the natural history of your region— and you should find a ready market.

Fantasy

Key your crafts to mythical medieval kingdoms ...the ancient mysteries of the Pyramids and the Sphinx...the wonders that lie waiting beyond the solar system. Or use your own imagination to create an entirely new fantasy!

And more

Professional forecasters charge big fees for helping corporations identify coming trends. You can have the same wonderful information for about $25 by purchasing one of author Faith Popcorn's bestselling books. Some of the trends she identified in *The Popcorn Report* (Doubleday): latchkey kids, log cabin chic, professional women at home, DOBYs (daddy older, baby younger).

pricing

OW THAT YOU have created samples of your first production designs, you are ready to determine their price. The heart of any craft artist's production line lies in works that wholesale for between $15 and $25. (Why? Because most holiday and birthday gift items are priced between $30 and $50.) Start with a few good products in this price range. Add a few more expensive and less expensive items, and you have the beginnings of a part-time or full-time studio! The most common error beginners make is to underprice their items. It's very easy to underestimate the time you will spend with a customer and the cost of advertising or selling as well as the time it takes to make an item. And don't forget profit!

SALE PRICE

	Retail	Wholesale
Production & Labor	$33	$33
Overhead & Selling Costs	$120	$33
Total Cost	$153	$66
Selling Price	$200	$100
Minus Costs	$153	$66
Profit	$47	$33

The Components of Pricing

Overhead cost

This includes the cost of utilities, rent, professional services (lawyer, bookkeeper and accountant), membership dues, books and periodicals.

Materials cost

Estimate your materials cost per item based on the lowest possible price available from suppliers. You may need to buy by the dozen, or even by the gross, to achieve the lowest materials cost.

Production cost

This is the cost of labor and materials for each item you produce. To start out, pay yourself $15 per hour. When your business grows you may choose to pay an assistant at a lower rate per hour to help with production. Production, materials and overhead costs together should not exceed

one-third of your wholesale price or 60% of your retail price. Keeping your retail selling costs below 60% is the hardest part of the equation.

Selling cost

If you sell your craftwork at a retail fair, the cost of the sale includes show fees, utilities, packing supplies, freight, travel expenses, display materials, and even the cost of your time and energy to sell your own work. It is important to analyze your selling costs with every show where you exhibit. Often your selling costs will exceed the 60% mark and eat into your profit too much.

If you sell through a store or boutique, the shop owner pays for advertising and displaying your work. Therefore, your selling costs are lower for a wholesale item than for an item you sell at retail at a craft fair. Selling costs for an item you retail yourself could be as high as 50% to 60% of the retail price! Selling costs should not exceed one-third of your wholesale price. Every time a store reorders by phone or mail, your selling costs are just pennies. Although your profit on each item might be a little lower, your risk is greatly reduced.

Profit

Most people think profit is something you put into the bank after a hard week's work. Wrong! Profit is the money you use to grow your business. You'll use profit to buy supplies for next month's production, pay in advance for booth fees and invest in new tools to make work easier and faster. Profit should be about 33 cents of every dollar you make.

networking

IT'S A PROVEN fact that craftspeople are more likely to succeed if they are part of a good, supportive network of other artists. Here are the best ways to find your peers.

Join the club

In 1995 the International Bead Conference had more than 1,000 attendees. The Woodturning Society has more than 7,000 members. The Glass Arts Society's membership roster has grown to 1,700 and the National Council on Education for the Ceramic Arts' to 2,500. There is surely an association for your craft; you will find a list in the Resources chapter at the end of this book.

Subscribe

Most magazines will put you in touch with important resources like workshops, conferences, exhibitions, competitions for cash awards—even shop owners who could be interested in your work. Some possibilities (addresses and phone numbers are in Resources):

AmericanStyle will help you find more than 500 craft gallery shows, museum exhibits, special craft events, festivals and fairs. In each issue you'll experience a city gallery crawl and visit the home of a passionate collector.

The Crafts Report is considered the Wall Street Journal of the crafts community, offering business advice and resources for professional artists in every medium.

Sunshine Artist covers the craft fair scene from malls to the better outdoor shows. It includes regional reports from around the country.

Ceramics Monthly focuses on technique but also lists workshops, exhibitions and calls for entry.

NICHE is read by more than 25,000 craft shop owners and lists calls for entry in all media.

Don't have time to read? Busy people keep magazines by the bed or in the briefcase. Just five minutes of reading a few times a day can help you cover mountains of material!

Find a group

Your state, regional or local craft guild is a great resource. Guilds provide seminars and workshops, the chance to meet other artists and mentors, exhibition opportunities, even group health insurance. Some guilds require an application, while others may only ask you to pay the annual dues. Guilds are listed in the Resources chapter.

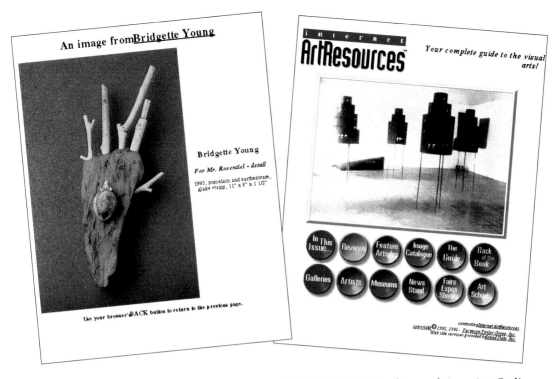

An image from Bridgette Young

Bridgette Young

For Mr. Rosentiel - detail

1995, porcelain and earthenware,
glaze stains, 11" x 8" x 1 1/2"

Use your browser's BACK button to return to the previous page.

internet
ArtResources

Your complete guide to the visual arts!

In This Issue... · Reviews · Feature Articles · Image Catalogue · The Guide · Back of the Book

Galleries · Artists · Museums · News Stand · Fairs Expos Shows · Art Schools

copyright © 1995, 1996 - Ferguson-Taylor Group, Inc.
Web site services provided by Round Data, Inc.

Find a place to learn

In many areas studio spaces have been developed by artists who prefer to work in a community instead of isolation. There is no substitute for the learning experiences you can gather from a small group of people with common interests, needs and problems. Again, see Resources for a list.

Find a resource organization

Beyond your state guild or local craft group are national organizations that help craftspeople and studio artists with difficult questions and decisions, and you will find a list in the Resources chapter. In addition, at least one national hotline handles craft business questions; call The Rosen Group at 1.800.43.CRAFT.

Find a mentor

A mentor is someone who will take a real interest in your progress...who will be happy to go to lunch at least once a month to talk about anything and everything. Your mentor should be two steps (or more) ahead of you on the path. The relationship can begin with just an invitation to lunch—where you will pick up the tab in return for truly valuable consulting.

Get on-line

Computer services like Compuserve (GOCRAFT), Prodigy and America Online provide great opportunities to chat with craftspeople from all around the country. The best way to start a conversation is to leave a message that asks a question. You'll get lots of advice, and sometimes conflict between your on-line mentors! Some craft forums have special sections for craft businesses and suppliers.

Use the Internet

Imagine typing in the words "stained-glass supplies" and getting back a list of hundreds of suppliers in less than 10 seconds! That's what the Internet is all about. Got a problem with a special type of paint or glue? Find the answer on the Net. Looking for craft fairs to visit when you take a vacation to California? That's on the Net, too. The Internet may not be the best place to sell your work (yet!), but it has a real talent for solving your problems.

Used computers can sell for as low as a few hundred dollars in newspaper classified ads. A modem is only a hundred dollars more. With simple business software like "Mind Your Own Business," you'll have consultants and resources at hand day or night.

Selling your own work is probably one of the hardest things you'll ever learn to do. It's easy to sell when there is no personal involvement...but your craftwork is so much a part of you that you may feel like you're selling an arm or leg!

It does take time to become comfortable with selling your work. Sometimes a friend can write better words for your brochure or be a better salesperson at a retail fair. Sometimes a customer can give you a perspective on your work that helps you market more effectively. Experiment to find what's right for you, and someday you'll find you actually enjoy the challenges of marketing.

Learning where to sell is as important—and as difficult—as learning how. The right retail craft fair, for example, is probably the best way to test market your work. But the wrong retail craft fair can be the fastest way to go out of business! This chapter gives you a guide to the types of sales settings available for fine crafts, with practical advice on each.

4
great
marketing
techniques

retail craft fairs

EACH YEAR THERE are more than 50,000 craft fairs, art festivals, bazaars and other opportunities to sell your work. Selecting the right ones is more than just luck. It requires research on your part, such as talking to other artists and craft enthusiasts to find out how well your work will fit and how much you can expect to earn. Probably 70% of the shows in your area won't even produce enough sales to meet your expenses!

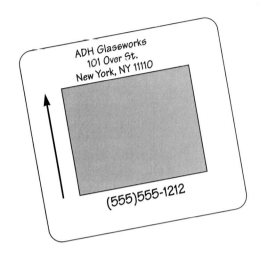

ADH Glassworks
101 Over St.
New York, NY 11110

(555)555-1212

on the retail craft fair circuit. If your work sells for $30 or more, you might be able to increase your sales by as much as 30% by allowing customers to use credit cards for their purchases. In general, good local fairs will offer you sales of $2,000-plus. There are about three dozen mega-fairs across the nation where average sales per artist can exceed $8,000!

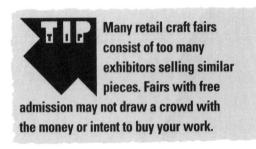

TIP Many retail craft fairs consist of too many exhibitors selling similar pieces. Fairs with free admission may not draw a crowd with the money or intent to buy your work.

Most of the better craft fairs and festivals select participants through a jury of artists and professionals who will grade your work against other applicants in your category. To enter, you usually submit a portfolio of color slides with your application. There is no substitute for good slides.

Many good artists are rejected or waitlisted for shows because their slides are below par—not necessarily bad, just ordinary. A good slide shows accurate color, texture and depth, as well as a gradient gray background with little or no shadow. You need a professional to produce this quality. Choose a commercial product photographer (not a portrait or wedding photographer). The cost will be over $500, but it is by far your best sales investment.

Credit cards offer you another competitive edge

wholesale craft shows

ASK YOURSELF: Which do I like best? A. Making craftwork. B. Selling my craftwork. If you answered "A," then wholesaling is the way to go!

At a wholesale craft show, the public (that is, the retail customer) is not invited. Instead, your customers are primarily owners of retail craft galleries and shops. Also attending...department store buyers, catalog companies, even Disney and QVC buyers. These buyers are well-educated retailers with an understanding of quality and uniqueness. Your goal is to create long-term relationships that will keep orders coming in with lit-tle additional effort or expense. Wholesaling gives you more time at home and in the studio.

There are regional and state wholesale craft shows as well as shows based on a specific type of style contemporary, mixed or country crafts. At the largest shows, exhibitors are divided by media or product type to help retailers scout out new work and buy one category at a time.

The largest national wholesale trade show devoted exclusively to craft artists is the Philadelphia Buyers Market of American Craft. Located in the Pennsylvania Convention Center, it is the largest craft show in the world. Each

February more than 1,500 artists from every state in the U.S. and Canada exhibit their wares to nearly 10,000 galleries, museum shops, department stores and specialty retailers. (A second show is held each summer.) If you want to meet buyers from Disney, QVC, Neiman Marcus, Bloomingdale's and the Smithsonian Museum Shops, this is the place.

Exhibitors are divided into sections for glass, ceramics, fashion, fine jewelry, fashion jewelry, interiors and kaleidoscopes. A mixed-media category includes wood, paper, baskets and other media. The show sponsors educational programs and provides child care for buyers and exhibitors.

The Philadelphia Buyers Market is sponsored by The Rosen Group, Inc., 3000 Chestnut Ave., Suite 300, Baltimore MD 21211, telephone 410.889.2933.

what to pack for a show

Following is a checklist of the things you will need for a good presentation at a craft show. You should also consider a display canopy for outdoor fairs, to keep the rain and the sun's glare off your work.

___ Booth Display
___ Extension Cords (30 ft.)
___ 2 Chairs
___ Lighting
___ Surge Protector
___ Trash Can
___ Tarp (Night Cover)
___ Display Accessories
___ Plate Stands
___ Packing Tape
___ Duct Tape
___ Light Bulbs
___ Glass Cleaner
___ Tool Box
___ First Aid Kit
___ Office Supplies
___ Credit Card Equipment

___ Cash Box
___ Petty Cash ($40)
___ Hand Vacuum
___ Receipt Book
___ Guest Book
___ Business Cards
___ Price Tags
___ Hang Tags
___ Retail Order Forms
___ Retail Price Lists
___ Promotionals
___ "See my work at..." Sign
___ Steamer or Iron
___ Thermos & Cooler
___ Other_____

gift & trade shows

YOU WILL find gift & trade shows in nearly every large city in the country. Shows with large craft sections include those in Atlanta, Chicago, San Francisco and New York.

Most smaller gift shows have craft sections, too, but with mixed success. Each show is very different. Visit those in your area, and talk to other artists about their experiences. Before you decide to apply, research whether the buyers who attend would be interested in your work. Show promoters rarely have sales statistics for prospective exhibitors.

The cost of an average booth ranges from $800 to $3,000, depending on the show and the number of amenities included in the exhibitor package.

There are many kinds of trade shows: furniture, bath, bridal, gifts, jewelry, fashions, fabric, accessories, quilts, holiday themes, lighting, gems, American crafts and more. The Resources chapter at the end of this book has a list of the larger gift & trade show promoters.

 TIP Most trade & gift show exhibitors offer imports that can compete with your product at a much lower price. Customers are often seeking products that will sell for under $20 (wholesale $8 to $10).

direct mail & catalog

THE DIRECT mail and catalog highway is littered with the bones of those who have gone before you!

There are, however, low-risk and no-risk ways to begin selling your work by direct mail. Take small steps (especially at first) and learn as you go.

Steps to Direct Mail Success

Step 1

Every successful direct mail effort begins with a very special list: yours! Collect the names and addresses of customers from checks, invoices and sales slips. This is your "A" or Active list. This list will always be your most profitable, because people who have bought from you before are likely to buy again.

Most businesses are built on the 80/20 rule: 80% of your sales come from 20% of your customers. Treat those customers like they are golden.

Step 2

Collect the names of possible future customers—that is, people who have seen your work and admired it. Always give people visiting your exhibit a chance to sign a guest book and include an address for future mailings.

Step 3

With each sale include a small re-order brochure. Full-color brochures work best, and the cost is small compared to the response they generate.

Step 4

Exchange names with another craft artist who has a successful direct mail list. (Note: not just a customer list.)

People who buy by mail are often not the same ones who buy in person.

Step 5

Track all sales to their source. When your customers call,

WILDER DESIGNS WHOLESALE ORDER FORM

SOLD TO:

SHIP TO:

TEL:

CONTACT:

DATE OF ORDER

DATE REQUIRED   SALES REP

P.O. #

TERMS: ☐ COD ☐ PROFORMA

THE GARDEN COLLECTION

VERDI	LEAD	QUANTITY RUST	MARBLE	BRONZE	CODE	DESCRIPTION	UNIT PRICE	TOTAL
					100	BUNNY *stake*	16.00	
					101	LILY FROG *stake*	13.00	
					200	SUN *plaque* (12½" D)	34.00	
					201	ST. FRANCIS *plaque*	34.00	
					202	LOVE BIRDS *plaque*	24.00	
					203	LEAPING FISH *plaque*	25.00	
					204	NOAH'S ARK *plaque*	50.00	
					205	PRIMAVERA *plaque*	50.00	
					206	ST. FIACRE *plaque*	50.00	
					207	NAPPING CAT *plaque*	6.00	
					208	SOL *plaque* (29" D)	120.00	
					209	JONAH & THE WHALE *plaque*	105.00	
					210	LARGE FEEDER W/BIRD *plaque*	45.00	
					211	SMALL FEEDER W/BIRD *plaque*	15.00	
					212	SMALL FEEDER W/SUN *plaque*	14.00	
					213	SUN/WELCOME *plaque*	9.25	
					214	BIRD & LEAF/WELCOME *plaque*	17.00	
					215	DRAGONFLY/WELCOME *plaque*	14.00	
					302	BUNNY *sculpture*	7.00	
					303	FROG *sculpture*	5.00	
					304	TROUT *sculpture*	14.50	
					305	RED DRUM *sculpture*	14.50	
						SUBTOTAL		

SIGNATURE:

Minimum order $150. Minimum reorder $100. Handling fee of $10 on any order not meeting minimum. All shipments COD. $4.50 COD charge paid by **Wilder Designs** on orders of $150. Shipping charges responsibility of buyer. Prices subject to change at any time.

WILDER DESIGNS
2336 Mt. Vernon Church Road, Raleigh, North Carolina 27614
919-848-3639 • Fax: 919-848-3624

---

ask where they found out about you. Put a small code on postcards and brochures so that you know where the sale came from. Also code customers by source in your database.

Step 6

Sell your work through direct mail catalogs like Smith & Hawkins, Lost Places or Sundance. Try to package a bounceback with your product. A bounceback can take the form of a registration card guarantee, collector's club membership or free newsletter offer, just to name a few. This will allow you to capture the names of the customers who have purchased your work.

Step 7

Print your own catalog and offer it for sale or free to a targeted audience. Printing a full color catalog can be as inexpensive as $500 or as expensive as $1 each. Color photocopies are efficient for a wholesale catalog targeted to retail store owners. Some retail craft catalogs are advertised in the classified sections of major magazines like *Southern Living, Architectural Digest, Smithsonian* and *The New Yorker.*

Taking the Catalog Gamble

Want to start your own catalog? Before you do, consider the following. Catalog companies are happy when they can make a $50 sale to only three people in every 200.

It usually costs $340 just to put a catalog in the mail to those 200 names. Getting $150 back means a loss of $190, multiplied many times over the entire mailing list.

Why do they do it? Catalog companies make money on "multi-buyers"—people who will always order from them. Only when the multi-buyers reach a certain level does the company turn a profit.

You can get more information on direct mail from the Direct Mail Marketing Association and *Catalog Age* magazine.

advertising

MAGAZINES, NEWSPAPERS, television, the telephone Yellow Pages and radio are powerful allies for any business. Researched thoroughly and used correctly, they can bring amazing results!

Newspapers

Best for announcing studio open houses and gallery receptions. They're also great for touting your accomplishments.

Every newspaper editor wants to run stories about local residents—in fact, the paper's success is often measured by the number of local names in each issue. Call or send a fax to get an expression of interest.

Magazines

These are divided into two basic types.

Consumer magazines reach either the general public or special-interest customers. Trade magazines cover professions and career fields. Craft and art gallery owners

Lewis + Hubener jewelry is available at the following fine galleries:

Real Mother Goose
901 SW Yamhill
Portland OR 97205
503-223-9510
Portland Airport
Washington Square

Lewis + Hubener
Sterling Silver and 18kt Vermeil Jewelry

Something/Anything
900 Northpoint - Ghirardelli Square
San Francisco CA 94109
415-441-8003

Wake Up Little Suzie
3409 Connecticut Ave NW
Washington DC 20008
202-244-0700

have their own "trades." The Rosen Group publishes two craft-related magazines. NICHE is a trade magazine for the owners of shops and galleries that carry American crafts; AMERICANSTYLE is a consumer magazine for collectors and admirers of craft arts. Both offer advertisers several choices: traditional display ads, co-op ads taken out by a group of artists and featuring all of them (or taken out by an artist and the gallery that shows the work) and "advertorials," which include a photograph of the artist's work and information on how to make contact, presented in an editorial format. You may choose to advertise in these trades as well as magazines with special-interest subscribers you want to reach.

Television

One of the newest and most effective ways to sell. The QVC shopping channel has a tradition of featuring the work of artists, craftspeople and other home-based businesses. Each of its special two-hour craft programs rings up sales of over $500,000! The channel also has a road show called "The Quest for America's Best," which goes from state to state to present crafts, specialty foods and other products from small local businesses.

Standard Rate and Data Services has directories of magazines, newspapers, radio and television rates and demographics.

open house events & studio tours

TO MANY OF YOUR customers, you are a mystery. What is it like to be an artist? How does your creativity find expression in your workplace and your lifestyle?

Open your house or studio, and give your customers and neighbors a chance to satisfy their curiosity. Of course, what everyone will see is far from the realities of daily life: The studio will be tidy and the kitchen spotless, with a platter of gourmet cookies and hot mulled cider on the stove. The living room will be picture perfect, with your work displayed to best advantage. Just another day at home? No, but a great selling opportunity!

If other artists live in your community or have studio space near yours, hold a multi-studio tour and turn it into a real occasion. If you time your event for just before the holiday season, guests will be in a mood to spend for beautiful handmade gifts. (A week or two before Thanksgiving works best, because it doesn't conflict with busy December schedules.)

When you join with other artists to create an event, be sure to advertise in local media and provide consumers with a brochure mapping out the location of other open studios.

If you live in a small town, the newspaper, TV and radio stations may take an interest in your event—with a little encouragement.

selling to stores & galleries

Cooperatives

You may not be ready (yet!) for sole proprietorship. But thousands of successful cooperative galleries have been started by a few enterprising artists who banded together to showcase their work. Retailers have an old saying that the three most important rules for success are "location, location and location." Don't forget that as you start to look for your own spot.

Every real estate developer dreams about finding elegant shops for tenants. You may be able to persuade a landlord that letting you test the waters in a new shopping area by giving you a reduced-cost lease will attract other upscale shops.

More tips for finding a good retail space:

■ Hot locations are near yuppie bookstores and

fancy dry cleaners. Gourmet coffee shops also make good neighbors.

■ Strip shopping centers anchored by super markets are often not worth the extra cost.

■ If you plan to locate near a movie theater or restaurant, you should be willing to stay open late for browsers.

■ After you close for the day, a timer will keep the front window or store lights on for extended hours. It's inexpensive advertising.

Sometimes you can create a wonderful environment with an old stand-alone house on a busy street in a retail zone. With eyecatching sculptures, windsocks, flowers and colorful porch furniture, you can create drama and excitement that's like a fancy lure to a hungry fish! Locations like these are often the most successful, especially when they come with low rent and good parking.

Before you make a commitment to any location, spend a weekday and a Saturday analyzing the foot traffic, the types of customers—and whether the customers are carrying purchases out of the shops!

Sub-Let Shops

One of Japan's most time-honored traditions has finally come to America: Retail stores will actually rent you a shelf for a monthly fee. You are required to provide the merchandise at no charge, but you will make more than the traditional 100% mark-up when an item is sold.

This strategy lets retailers reluctant to buy new artists' work lower their risk, which could make the difference in their willingness to showcase your crafts. You gain more control over pricing, display, lighting and advertising without the day-

to-day responsibility of opening the store and waiting for customers.

Hundreds of sub-let shops concentrate on country and hobby-type production crafts. Just a few galleries work with limited-production and one-of-a-kind works at higher price levels. It's best to live near the shop and visit often to analyze what is selling and how often the display needs work.

Guild Shops

Nearly every state has at least one store sponsored by a regional guild. The largest one in the country is Tamarack: The Best of West Virginia, which opened in June 1996 in Beckley. More than 10,000 products made by state residents are displayed in the 59,000-square-foot facility, which is also home to studios, training and apprenticeship programs, workshops, cultural exhibits and a theater.

Also quite large is the Southern Highland Craft Guild's Allanstand store in Asheville, N.C. Its location on the Blue Ridge Parkway brings visits from nearly a million tourists each year.

Some guilds will buy your work for 50% of the retail price. Others will take your work on consignment, offering you 50% to 60% of the retail price when the item is sold.

A list of some of these shops is in the guild section of the Resources chapter at the back of the book.

resources

GUILDS/ORGANIZATIONS

Albermarle Craftsman's Guild
P.O. Box 1301
Elizabeth City NC 27909

Albuquerque Arts Alliance
20 First Plaza
Albuquerque NM 87102
505.243.4971

American Art Pottery Association
125 E. Rose
Webster Groves MO 63119
314.968.0708

American Arts and Craft Alliance, Inc.
425 Riverside Dr., #15H
New York NY 10025
212.866.2239

American Association of Woodturners
667 Harriet Ave.
Shoreview MN 55126
612.484.9094

American Blacksmith Society
P.O. Box 977
Peralta NM 87042

American Craft Association
21 S. Eltings Corner Rd.
Highland NY 12528
800.724.0859

American Craft Museum
40 W. 53rd St.
New York NY 10019-6112
212.956.6047

**American Furniture
Manufacturers Association**
P.O. Box HP-7
High Point NC 27261
919.884.5000

American Needlepoint Guild
79 N. Floral Leaf Cir.
The Woodlands TX 77381
409.321.3872

American Quilter's Society
P.O. Box 3290
Paducah KY 42001
502.898.7903

American Society of Interior Designers
608 Massachusetts Ave. N.E.
Washington DC 20002
202.546.3480

Appalachian By Design
Center for Economic Options
Lewisburg WV 24901
304.647.3455

Arizona Clay
45 W. Lynnwood
Phoenix AZ 85003
602.254.1222

Arizona Commission on the Arts
417 W. Roosevelt Ave.
Phoenix AZ 85003
602.255.5882

Arizona Designer Craftsmen
136 E. Voltaire
Phoenix AZ 85022
602.863.1212

Arizona Woodworkers Association
1821 N. Meadowlark Dr.
Flagstaff AZ 86001
520.774.3270

Arkansas Arts Council
1500 Tower Bldg.
323 Center St.
Little Rock AR 72201
501.324.9150

Arkansas Craft Guild
P.O. Box 800
Mountain View AR 75260
501.746.4396

Artisans Center
334 Wichman St.
Walterboro SC 29488
803.549.0011

**Artist-Blacksmiths' Association
of North America**
P.O. Box 1181
Nashville TN 47449
812.988.6919

Artlink, Inc.
P.O. Box 3426
Phoenix AZ 85030
602.256.7539

Arts Council of New Orleans
522 Baronne St., #1712
New Orleans LA 70112
504.523.1465

Arts Extension Service
University of Massachusetts
Amherst MA 01003
413.545.2360

Blue Ridge Hearthside Crafts
Route 1, Box 738
Banner Elk NC 28604
704.963.5252

Bureau of Women's Business Development
400 Forum Bldg.
Harrisburg PA 17120
717.787.3339

Capitol Area Porcelain Guild
3358 Hampton Rd.
Raleigh NC 27607

Capitol Quilters Guild
2618 Wade Ave.
Raleigh NC 27606

Carolina Clay Guild
109 Kemp Rd. E., #E
Greensboro NC 27410

Carolina Designer Craftsmen
P.O. Box 33791
Raleigh NC 27636
919.460.1551

Catawba Valley Leathermen's Guild
P.O. Box 4095, Longview Branch
Hickory NC 28603
704.322.5350

Central Arizona Weavers and Spinners
392 W. Roosevelt
Coolidge AZ 85228

Charlotte Handweavers Guild
7200 Terrace Dr.
Charlotte NC 28211

City of Irving Arts Board
3333 N. MacArthur, #300
Irving TX 75062-7417
214.252.7558

Coastal Carolina Fiber Guild
703 Riverhills Dr.
Greenville NC 27843

College Art Association
275 Seventh Ave., 5th Floor
New York NY 10001
212.691.1051

Connecticut Guild of Craftsmen
P.O. Box 155
New Britain CT 06050
860.225.8875

Core Sound Decoy Carvers Guild
P.O. Box 308
Harkers Island NC 28531

Craft Alliance of Missouri
6640 Delmar Blvd.
St Louis MO 63130
314.725.1177

Craft Emergency Relief Fund
P.O. Box 838
Montpelier VT 05601
802.229.2306

Crafts Center
1001 Connecticut Ave. N.W., #1138
Washington DC 20036
202.728.9603

Embroiderer's Guild of America
335 W. Broadway, #100
Louisville KY 40202
502.589.6956

Empire State Crafts Alliance
320 Montgomery St.
Syracuse NY 13202
518.584.1819

Enamel Guild Northeast
197 Nomoco Rd.
Freehold NJ 07728
908.577.0179

Enamelist Society
P.O. Box 310
Newport KY 41072
606.291.3800

Farmington Valley Art Center
25 Arts Center Ln.
Avon CT 06001
860.678.1867

Fiber Artists of Dallas
3908 Mission Ridge
Plano TX 75023

Fiber Arts Guild
P.O. Box 27501
Las Vegas NV 89126

First Nations Development Institute
11917 Main St.
Fredericksburg VA 22408-7326
540.371.5615

Florida Craftsmen
501 Central Ave.
St. Petersburg FL 33701
813.821.7391

Fountain Hills Art League
14610 N. Valloroso Dr.
Fountain Hills AZ 85268

Friendship Spinners
2134 Belmont Rd.
Louisville KY 40218

Gem Cutters Guild of Baltimore
3600 Clipper Mill Rd., #116
Baltimore MD 21211

Glass Arts Society
1305 Fourth Ave., #711
Seattle WA 98101-2401
206.382.1305

Greater Columbus Arts Council
55 E. State St.
Columbus OH 43215
614.224.2606

Greater Harrisburg Arts Council
444 S. Second St.
Harrisburg PA 17104
717.238.5180

Greenville Quilters Guild
1701 Sulgrave
Greenville SC 27834

Handweavers Guild of America
3327 Duluth Hwy.
Duluth GA 30136
770.495.7702

Handweavers of America
630 E. Wesleyan Dr.
Tempe AZ 85282

High Country Art and Craft Guild
P.O. Box 2854
Asheville NC 28802
704.254.0072

Iredell County Craft Guild
1525 Melviney St.
Statesville NC 28677

Irving Art Association
P.O. Box 153581
Irving TX 75015
214.721.2488

Jewelers' Resource Bureau
2350 Broadway, #1011
New York NY 10024
212.580.4256

Kentucky Art and Craft Foundation
609 W. Main St.
Louisville KY 40202
502.589.0102

Kentucky Arts Council
31 Fountain Pl.
Frankfort KY 40601-1942
502.564.3757

Kentucky Center for the Arts
5 River Front Plaza
Louisville KY 40202
502.562.0100

Kentucky Citizens for the Arts
125 S. Seventh St.
Louisville KY 40202
502.589.3116

Kentucky Craft Marketing
39 Fountain Pl.
Frankfort KY 40601-1942
888.KY.CRAFT

Kentucky Folklife Program
Berea College
C.P.O. 760
Berea KY 40404
606.986.9341

Kentucky Guild of Artists and Craftspeople
P.O. Box 291
Berea KY 40403
606.986.3192

Kentucky Heritage Quilt Society
P.O. Box 23392
Lexington KY 40523

Kernersville Arts and Crafts Guild
P.O. Box 222
Kernersville NC 27284
910.996.0868

Knitting Guild of America
P.O. Box 1606
Knoxville TN 37901
423.524.2401

League of New Hampshire Craftsmen
205 N. Main St.
Concord NH 03301
603.224.3375

Lexington Arts and Cultural Center
161 N. Mill St.
Lexington KY 40507
606.233.1469

Lexington Embroiderer's Guild
117 Westwood Dr.
Richmond KY 40475
606.623.0703

Logan Lap Quilters
P.O. Box 7034
Columbia SC 29202

Louisville Craftmen's Guild
P.O. Box 7172
Louisville KY 40207
502.451.1424

Louisville Embroiderer's Guild
37 Hill Rd.
Louisville KY 40204
502.451.4399

Louisville Miniature Club
2936 Goose Creek Rd.
Louisville KY 40241
502.425.8608

Louisville Visual Art Association
275 Louisville Galleria
Louisville KY 40202
502.581.1445

Maco Crafts
2846 Georgia Rd.
Franklin NC 28734
704.524.7878

Maine Crafts Association
P.O. Box 228
Deer Isle ME 04627
207.348.9943

Manufacturing Jewelers and Silversmiths of America
1 State St., 6th Floor
Providence RI 02908
401.274.3840

Maryland Art Place
218 W. Saratoga St.
Baltimore MD 21201

Mesa Art League
2046 E St.
Gary Circle
Mesa AZ 85208
602.964.4508

Michigan Guild of Artists and Artisans
118 N. Fourth Ave.
Ann Arbor MI 48104
313.662.3382

Mid-Atlantic Arts Foundation
11 E. Chase St., #1A
Baltimore MD 21202
410.539.6656

Minnesota Crafts Council
528 Hennepin Ave., #216
Minneapolis MN 55403
612.333.7789

Minority Business Development Agency
14th St. and Constitution Ave., Room 5099
Washington DC 20230
202.482.4547

Montclair Craft Guild
P.O. Box 538
Glenridge NJ 07028
201.783.4110

Mothers Home Business Network
P.O. Box 423
East Meadow NY 11554
516.997.7394

Mountain Spinners and Weavers Guild
P.O. Box 1820
Prescott AZ 86302
520.778.1397

Movimiento Artistico del Rio Salado (MARS)
P.O. Box 20431
Phoenix AZ 85003
602.253.3541

Nantahala Fiber Guild
116 Bellview
Franklin NC 28734

Nashville Metro Arts Commission
209 10th Ave. S., #416
Nashville TN 37203-4101
615.862.6720

National Council on Education for the Ceramic Arts
P.O. Box 158
Bandon OR 97411
800.99.NCECA

National Guild of Community
Schools of the Arts
P.O. Box 8018
Englewood NJ 07631
201.871.3337

National Ornamental and
Miscellaneous Metals Association
804 Main St.
Forest Park GA 30050
404.363.4009

National Quilting Association
P.O. Box 393
Ellicott City MD 21041-0393
410.461.5733

National Terrazzo and Mosaic Association
3166 Des Plaines Ave., #12
Des Plaines IL 60018
847.635.7744

National Woodcarvers Association
7424 Miami Ave.
Cincinnati OH 45243
513.561.0627

Nevada Clay Arts Guild
1505 Westwood Dr.
Reno NV 89509

New Hampshire State Council on the Arts
40 N. Main St.
Concord NH 03301
603.271.2789

New Horizons Quilters
2012 St. Mary's St.
Raleigh NC 27608

New Jersey Designer Craftsmen
65 Church St.
New Brunswick NJ 08901-1242
908.246.4066

North Carolina Arts Council
221 E. Lane St.
Raleigh NC 27611
919.733.2111

North Carolina Crafts
409 W. Hill Ave.
Hillsborough NC 27278

North Carolina Quilt Symposium
727 Seneca Pl.
Charlotte NC 28210

North Carolina Society of Goldsmiths
c/o Ringmasters Jewelers
111G Reynolda Village
Winston-Salem NC 27106
910.722.2218

Oglebay Institute, Stifel Fine Arts Center
1330 National Rd.
Wheeling WV 26003

Ohio Designer Craftsmen
1665 W. Fifth Ave.
Columbus OH 43212
614.486.7119

Old 96 Basketmakers Guild
318 Port Royal Dr.
Ninety Six SC 29666

Ontario Crafts Council-Craft Gallery
35 McCaul St.
Toronto Ontario
CANADA M5T 1V7
416.977.3551

Ontario Handweavers and Spinners
35 McCaul St.
Toronto Ontario
CANADA M5T 1V7
416.971.9641

Orangeburg League of the Arts
6305 North Rd.
Orangeburg SC 29115
803.534.5966

Pennsylvania Guild of Craftsmen
P.O. Box 108
State College PA 16804
814.238.5538

Pennyroyal Crafts Group
P.O. Box 1176
Hopkinsville KY 42241
502.271.2989

Perquimans Quilters Club
P.O. Box 87
Hertford NC 27944

Peters Valley Craft Center
19 Kuhn Rd.
Layton NJ 07851
201.948.5200

Philadelphia Office of Arts and Culture
1600 Arch St., 12th Floor
Philadelphia PA 19103
215.686.8684

Phoenix City Arts Center
1202 N. Third St.
Phoenix AZ 85004
602.262.4627

Phoenix Commission on the Arts
200 W. Washington St.
Phoenix AZ 85003-1611
602.262.4637

Piedmont Craftsmen
1204 Reynolda Rd.
Winston-Salem NC 27104
910.725.1516

Piedmont Hotwheels Handspinners
623 Infinity Rd.
Durham NC 27712

Piedmont Woodcarvers
Route 7, Box 234
Mooresville NC 28115

Pine Tree Quilters
405 Pine Hill Dr
Wilmington NC 28403

Planters Craftsmen Guild
P.O. Box 1220
Rocky Mount NC 27802-1220
919.442.0181

Poor Folk Art and Crafts Guild
309 W. Main St.
Cumberland KY 40823
606.589.2496

Potters Guild of Baltimore
Meadow Mill, Suite 101
Baltimore MD 21211
410.235.4884

Prescott Valley Art Guild
P.O. Box 26577
Prescott Valley AZ 86312

Princeton Art Guild
115 E. Main St.
Princeton KY 42445
502.365.3959

Prince George's Arts Council
6611 Kenilworth Ave., #200
Riverdale MD 20737
301.324.1455

Pyramid Atlantic Center for Papermaking
6001 66th Ave., #103
Riverdale MD 20737
301.459.7154

Raleigh Craft Club
1212 Park Ave.
Garner NC 27529

Raleigh Miniatures Guild
5519 Parkwood Dr.
Raleigh NC 2761

Randolph Quilters Guild
P.O. Box 2664
Asheboro NC 27204

Reno Fiber Guild
P.O. Box 12662
Reno NV 89510
817.658.4084

Scottsdale Artists' League
11614 N. 68th Pl.
Scottsdale AZ 85253
602.948.2447

Seacoast Spinners and Weavers Guild
P.O. Box 194
Atlantic NC 2851

Seashore Weavers and Spinners
813 Santa Maria
Wilmington NC 2840

Silversmiths of America
1 State St., 6th Floor
Providence RI 02908-5035

Small Business Administration
1110 Vermont Ave. NW, 9th Floor
Washington DC 20043
202.606.4000

Smocking Arts Guild
2501 Brentwood Dr.
Carson City NV 89701

Smokey Mountain Fiber Guild
P.O. Box 1207
Cullowhee NC 28723

Smokey Mountain Quilters Guild
P.O. Box 1381
Franklin NC 28734

Society of American Silversmiths
P.O. Box 3599
Cranston RI 02910
401.461.3156

Society of Arts and Crafts
175 Newbury St.
Boston MA 02116

Society of North American Goldsmiths
2202 Camino Rancho Siringo
Santa Fe NM 87505
505.471.1014

South Carolina Art Guild
P.O. Box 7391
Columbia SC 29202
803.786.3839

South Carolina Crafts Association
P.O. Box 6963
Columbia SC 29260

Southeastern Fiber Guild
7976 Market St.
Wilmington NC 28405

Southern Arizona Clay Artists
P.O. Box 44218
Tucson AZ 85733
520.888.8297

Southern Highland Handcraft Guild
P.O. Box 9545
Asheville NC 28815
704.298.7928

Southern Home Furnishings Association
P.O. Box 1259
High Point NC 27260
800.274.7432

Southwest Craft Center
300 Augusta
San Antonio TX 78205
210.224.1848

Southwestern Artists Association
P.O. Box 483
Prescott AZ 86302

Southwestern League of Fine Arts
P.O. Box 30758
Tucson AZ 85751

Spectral Artists
1443 N. 61st Pl.
Mesa AZ 85205
602.981.6776

Spin Off
1121 Fenimore St.
Winston-Salem NC 27103

Stained Glass Association of America
6 S.W. Second St., #7
Lee's Summit MO 64063
816.524.9340

Stone Mountain Crafts
Route 1, Box 59
Traphill NC 28685

Sun City Handweavers and Spinners Guild
16820 N. 99th Ave.
Sun City AZ 85351
602.974.8925

Surface Design Association
P.O. Box 20799
Oakland CA 94620
707.829.3110

Tarheel Quilters Guild
616 Levenhall Rd.
Fayetteville NC 2831

Tarheel Tolers
2301 Beechridge Rd.
Raleigh NC 2760

Tarheel Woodcarvers Association
301 Wesley Dr.
Givens Estates
Asheville NC 28803

Telarana Weavers and Spinners Guild
P.O. Box 41832
Mesa AZ 85274-1832
602.962.0603

Tempe Art League
P.O. Box 24891
Tempe AZ 85285-4891
602.276.8904

Texas Area Artists
P.O. Box 515204
Dallas TX 75251
214.239.9294

Texas Arts Commission
P.O. Box 13406
Austin TX 78711-3406
512.463.5535

Texas Visual Arts Association
2207 Spanish Trail
Arlington TX 76013
817.461.1525

Three Rivers Quilt Guild
8962 Whitley Rd.
Norwood NC 28128

Torpedo Factory Art Center
105 N. Union St.
Alexandria VA 22314
703.838.4565

Trenholm Artist Guild
8 Westlake Rd.
Columbia SC 2920

Triangle Potters Guild
P.O. Box 10161
Raleigh NC 27605

Triangle Weavers
P.O. Box 3055
Chapel Hill NC 27515

Truckee Meadows Quilters
4300 Acacia Way
Reno NV 89502

Tryon Crafts
P.O. Box 1245
Tryon NC 28782
704.859.8323

Tucson Arts Coalition
P.O. Box 43160
Tucson AZ 85733

Tucson Handweavers and Spinners
5644 E. Ninth St.
Tucson AZ 85711
520.745.6054

Uwharrie Spinsters
P.O. Box 302
Climax NC 27233

Vermont State Craft Center at Frog Hollow
1 Mill St.
Middlebury VT 05753
802.388.3177

Virginia Coop Extension Service
P.O. Box 9081
Petersburg VA 23806

Waccamaw Arts and Crafts Guild
P.O. Box 1595
Myrtle Beach SC 29578

Wake Weavers Guild
1408 Lorimer Rd.
Raleigh NC 27606

Washtenaw Council for the Arts
P.O. Box 8154
Ann Arbor MI 48107
313.484.4882

Wayne Spinners Guild
619 Park Ave. Goldsboro NC 27530

Wesleyan Potters
350 S. Main St.
Middletown CT 06457
860.347.5925

West Valley Artists, Inc.
c/o 11217 W. Ashbrook Pl.
Avondale AZ 85323
602.877.9113

**West Virginia Division of
Culture and History**
State Capital Complex
Charleston WV 25305
304.558.0220

**Western North Carolina Fibers/
Handweavers Guild**
P.O. Box 233
Flat Rock NC 28731

Wilmington Craft Guild
422 Kelly Rd.
Wilmington NC 28409

Winston-Salem Fiber Guild
600 N. Trade St.
Winston-Salem NC 27101

Woman Kraft
388 S. Stone Ave.
Tucson AZ 85701-2318

Woodchucks
P.O. Box 20237
Sun Valley NV 89433

Woodworkers Guild of South Carolina
209 Argyll Rd.
Columbia SC 29210

Academy of Art College
Art Dept.
410 Bush St.
San Francisco CA 94108

Adams State College
Art Dept.
208 Edgemont
Alamosa CO 81102

Aims Community College
Art Dept.
Box 69
Greeley CO 80632

Alabama A & M
Dept. of Art and Art Education
Normal AL 35762

Albert Stained Glass Studio
57 Front St.
Brooklyn NY 11201

Albertson College
Art Dept.
2112 Cleveland Blvd.
Caldwell ID 83605

Alfred University
School of Art and Design
Alfred NY 14802

Amarillo College
Art Dept.
P.O. Box 447
2200 S. Washington
Amarillo TX 79178

American Institute of Diamond Cutting
1287 E. Newport Center Dr., #202
Deerfield Beach FL 33442-7706

American Jeweler's Institute
11904 S.E. Stark
Portland OR 97216

American River College
Art Dept.
4700 College Oak Dr.
Sacramento CA 95841

American Watchmaking Institute
10600 Springfield Pike
Cincinnati OH 45215

Anderson Ranch Arts Center
P.O. Box 5598
Snowmass CO 81615

Anderson University
Art Dept.
1100 E. Fifth St.
Anderson IN 46012

Appalachian Center for Crafts
1560 Craft Center Dr.
Smithville TN 37166

Argent Jeweler's Institute
6338 Vanderbilt Ave.
Dallas TX 75214-3366

Arizona State University
School of Art
Tempe AZ 85287-1505

Arkansas Art Center Museum School
P.O. Box 2137
Little Rock AR 72203

Arnstein Company
P.O. Box 1220
Mercer Island WA 98040

Arrowmont School for Crafts
P.O. Box 567
Gatlinburg TN 37738
423.436.5860

Art and Fashion Institute of Dallas
Art Dept.
2 N. Park E.
Dallas TX 75231-9959

The Art Institute
Art Dept.
1622 Chestnut St.
Philadelphia PA 19103

Art Institute of Boston
700 Beacon St.
Boston MA 02215

Art Institute of Chicago
37 S. Wabash, #707
Chicago IL 60603

Austin School of Jewelry Design
603 Baylor
Austin TX 78703

Bakersfield College
Art Dept.
1801 Panorama Dr.
Bakersfield CA 93305

Ball State University
Art Dept.
Muncie IN 47306

Bard College
Art Dept.
Annandale-on-the-Hudson NY 12504-5000

Baylor University
Art Dept.
Waco TX 76798-7263

Beaver College
Fine Arts Dept.
Easton and Church Rds.
Glenside PA 19038

Bellarmine College
Art Dept.
2001 Newburg Rd.
Louisville KY 40205-0671

Bemidji State University
Visual Arts Dept.
1500 Birchmont Dr.
Bemidji MN 56601-2699

Berea College
Art Dept.
C.P.O. Box 2347
Berea KY 40404

Berkshire Center for Contemporary Glass
6 Harris St.,Box 377
West Stockbridge MA 02160

Bethany College
Art Dept.
421 N. Olson
Lindsborg KS 67456

Birmingham Bloomfield Art Association
1516 S. Cranbrook Rd.
Birmingham ME 48009

**Bishop State Community
College, SW Campus**
Art Dept.
925 Dauphin Island Pkwy.
Mobile AL 36605-3299

Blair School for Jewelers
3621 Liberty Sq. Shopping Center
Boiling Springs SC 29316

Bloomsburg University
Art Dept.
Old Science Hall
Bloomsburg PA 17815

Blue Mountain Community College
Art Dept.
2411 N.W. Carden Ave.
Pendleton OR 97801

Blueberry Cove Foundation
300 Massachusetts Ave., #121
Arlington MA 02174

Boise State University
Art Dept.
1910 University Dr.
Boise ID 83725

Boston Architectural Center
320 Newbury St.
Boston MA 02115

Boston University
School of the Arts
855 Commonwealth Ave.
Boston MA 02215

Boston University Metropolitan College
Arts Administration Graduate Program
808 Commonwealth Ave., 2nd Floor
Boston MA 02215

Bowling Green State University
School of Art
1000 Fine Art Center
Bowling Green OH 43403

Bridgewater State College
Art Dept.
Bridgewater MA 02325

Brookfield Craft Center
P.O. Box 122, Rt. 25
Brookfield CT 06804

The Bryn Athyn College of the New Church
Art Dept.
P.O. Box 717
Bryn Athyn PA 19009

Bucks County Community College
Hicks Art Cir.
Swamp Rd.
Newton PA 18940

Bullseye Glass Company
3722 S.E. 21st Ave.
Portland OR 97202

Bulova School of Watchmaking
4024 62nd St.
Woodside NY 11377

SCHOOLS/ART CENTERS

C. Bauer Studio
214 W. 29th St., #1502
New York NY 1000

Cabrillo College
Art Dept.
6500 Soquel Dr.
Aptos CA 95003

California College of Arts and Crafts
5212 Broadway
Oakland CA 94618-1487

California Institute of Jewelry
420 El Camino Ave., #B1
Sacramento CA 95821

California Polytechnic State University
Dept. of Art and Design
San Luis Obispo CA 93407

California State University, Fullerton
Art Dept.
800 N. State College Blvd.
Fullerton CA 92634-9480

California State University, Fresno
Art and Design Dept.
5225 N. Backer Ave.
Fresno CA 93740

California State University, Long Beach
Art Dept.
1250 Bellflower Blvd.
Long Beach CA 90840

California State University, Los Angeles
Art Dept.
5151 State University Dr.
Los Angeles CA 90032

California State University, Northridge
School of the Arts
3-D Media Dept.
Northridge CA 91330

California State University, San Bernardino
Art Dept.
5500 University Pkwy.
San Bernardino CA 92407

California State University, Sacramento
Art Dept.
6000 J St.
Sacramento CA 95819-6061

**California State University/
San Francisco State University**
Art Dept.1600 Holloway Ave.
San Francisco CA 94132

California University of Pennsylvania
Dept. of Art
P.O. Box 33
California PA 15419

Capital University
Fine Arts Dept.
2199 E. Main St.
Columbus OH 43209

Cardinal Stritch College
Art Dept.
6801 Yates Rd.
Milwaukee WI 53217

Carleton College
Art Dept.
1 N. College St.
Northfield MN 55057

Carnegie Mellon University
Art Dept.
5000 Forbes Ave., #312
Pittsburgh PA 15213

Case Western Reserve University
Art Dept.
Wickenden Bldg.
Cleveland OH 44106

Casper College
Dept. of Visual Arts
125 College Dr.
Casper WY 82601

Cazenovia College
Fashion Design Program
P.O. Box P
Cazenovia NY 13035

Cedar Crest College
Art Dept.
100 College Dr.
Allentown PA 18104-6196

Center for Creative Studies
201 E. Kirby
Detroit MI 48202

Central Connecticut State University
Dept. of Art
1615 Stanley St.
New Britain CT 06050

Central Michigan University
Art Dept.
132 Wightman Hall
Mount Pleasant MI 48859

Central Oregon Community College
Art Dept.
2600 N.W. College Way
Bend OR 97701

Central Washington University
Art Dept.
Ellensburg WA 98926-7564

Centre College
Art Dept.
600 W. Walnut
Danville KY 40422

Cerritos College
Dept. of Art
11110 Alondra Blvd.
Norwalk CA 90650

Chadron State College
Art Dept.
Chadron NE 69337

Charles Stewart Mott Community College
Art Dept.
School of Arts and Humanities
1401 E. Court St.
Flint MI 48502

Chautauqua Institution
School of Art
P.O. Box 1098
Chautauqua NY 14722

Cheltenham Center for the Arts
Art Dept.
439 Ashbourne Rd.
Cheltenham PA 19012

Citrus College
Art Dept.
1000 W. Foothill
Glendora CA 91741

City College of San Francisco
Art Dept.
50 Phelan Ave.
San Francisco CA 94112

Clackamas Community College
Art Dept.
196000 S. Molalla
Oregon City OR 97045

Claremont School of Art
Art Dept.
251 E. 10th St.
Claremont CA 91711

Clarion University of Pennsylvania
Art Dept.
Clarion PA 16214

Clark College
Art Dept.
1800 E. McLoughlin Blvd.
Vancouver WA 98663

Cleveland Institute of Art
11141 E. Blvd., University Cir.
Cleveland OH 44106

Cline Glass
1135 S.E. Grand
Portland OR 97214

Cochise College
Art Dept.
4190 W. Hwy. 80
Douglas AZ 85607-9724

College of Dupage
Art Dept.
IC Bldg. 31258, Lambert Rd at 22nd St.
Glen Ellyn IL 60137

College of Marin
Dept. of Art
Kentfield CA 94904

College of Mount St. Joseph
Art Dept.
Delhi and Neeb Rds.
Cincinnati OH 45233-1670

College of New Rochelle
School of Arts and Sciences
New Rochelle NY 10805

College of St. Catherine
Art Dept.
20204 Randolph St.
Paul MN 55105

College of the Redwoods
Arts Dept.
7351 Tompkins Hill Rd.
Eureka CA 95501

Colorado State University
Dept. of Art
Visual Arts #G100
Fort Collins CO 80523

Columbus College of Art and Design
Art Dept.
107 N. 9th St.
Columbus OH 43215

Columbus State University
Art Dept.
4225 University Ave.
Columbus GA 31907-5645

Conner Jeweler's Institute
4820 University Dr., Suite 2
Huntsville AL 35816

Copley Society of Boston
158 Newbury St.
Boston MA 02116

Corning Museum Glass Studio
1 Museum Way
Corning NY 14830

Craft Business Institute
The Rosen Group
3000 Chestnut Ave., #300
Baltimore MD 21211

The Crafts Center
Cedar Lakes Conference Center
Ripley WV 25271

Cranbrook Academy of Art
1221 Woodward Ave., P.O. Box 801
Bloomfield Hills MI 48303

Creative Arts Workshop
80 Audubon St.
New Haven CT 06510

Creative Glass Center of America
1501 Glasstown Rd.
Millville NJ 08332

Creative Stained Glass Studio
85 S. Union Blvd., Unit C
Lakewood CO 80228-2207

Cypress College
Art Dept.
9200 Valley View St.
Cypress CA 90630

Dallas Jewelry Institute
2560 Electronic Ln., #107
Dallas TX 75220

Danforth Museum School
123 Union Ave.
Framingham MA 0170

Daytona Beach Community College
Continuing Education
P.O. Box 2811
Daytona Beach FL 33120-2811

Delaware State University
Dept. of Art and Art Education
1200 N. Dupont Hwy.
Dover DE 19901-2275

Drake University
Art Dept.
25th and Carpenter
Des Moines IA 50311

Drexel University
Nesbitt College of Design Arts
Philadelphia PA 19104

Dunconnor Workshops
P.O. Box 416
Salida CO 81201

East Carolina University
School of Art
E. Fifth St.
Greenville NC 27858-4353

East Tennessee State University
Art Dept.
P.O. Box 70078
Johnson City TN 37614

East Texas State University
Art Dept.
East Texas Station
Commerce TX 75429-3011

Eastern Arizona College
Art Dept.
600 Church St.
Thatcher AZ 85552

Eastern Kentucky University
Art Dept.
Campbell Bldg #309-3109
Richmond KY 40475

Eastern Kentucky University Tech Center
Art Dept.
307 Whalin Technology Complex
Richmond KY 40475-3131

Eastern Michigan University
Art Dept.
114 Ford
Ypsilanti MI 48197

Eastern New Mexico University
Art Dept.
Art and Education #19
Portales NM 88130

Eastern Oregon State College
Art Dept.
1410 L Ave.
La Grande OR 97850-2899

Eastfield College
Art Dept.
3737 Motley
Mesquite TX 75150

Echoes of the Renaissance
P.O. Box 1041
Stowe VT 05672

Edinboro University of PA
Art Dept
102 Doucette Hall
Edinboro PA 16444

El Camino College
Division of Fine Arts
16007 Crenshaw Blvd.
Torrance CA 90506

Elgin Community College
1700 Spartan Dr.
Elgin IL 60123

Elliott Bay Art Glass
Glass Art Dept.
904 Elliott Ave. W.
Seattle WA 98119

Emma Willard School
285 Pawling Ave.
Troy NY 12180

Emporia State University
Division of Art
1200 Commercial #4015
Emporia KS 66801-5087

Evergreen Valley College
Art Dept.
3095 Yerba Buena Rd.
San Jose CA 95135

Farrin & O'Connor Design Studio
146 W. Bellevue Dr.
Pasadena CA 91105

Fashion Institute of Technology
227 W. 27th St.
New York NY 10001-5992

Fenton Glass Studio
4001 San Leandro St., #8
Oakland CA 94601

Fine Arts Center
1613 W. Washington St.
Greenville SC 29601

Fine Arts Work Center
Summer Program
24 Pearl St.
Provincetown MA 02657

Florida Atlantic University
Art Dept.
777 Glades Rd.
Boca Raton FL 33431

Florida Gulf Coast Art Center
222 Ponce De Leon Blvd.
Belleair FL 34616

Florida International University
Visual Arts Dept.
University Park Campus, Bldg. DM383C
Tamiami Trail
Miami FL 33199

Foothills Artists
P.O. Box 264
White Oak KY 41472

Forest Hills Adult Center
Art Dept.
6701 110th St.
Forest Hills NY 11375

Fort Hays State University
Dept. of Art
600 Park St.
Hays KS 6760

Fort Lewis College
Art Dept.
1000 Rim Dr.
Durango CO 81301-3999

Franklin Pierce College
Art Dept
College Rd.
Rindge NH 03461

SCHOOLS/ART CENTERS

Friends University
Art Dept.
2100 University Ave.
Wichita KS 67213

Fullerton College
Art Dept.
321 E. Chapman Ave.
Fullerton CA 9263

Gem City College
Art Dept.
700 State St.,
P.O. Box 179
Quincy IL 62301

Gemological Institute of America
1660 Stewart St.
Santa Monica CA 90404-4088

Georgia Southwestern College
Art Dept.
800 Wheatley St.
Americus GA 31709

Georgia State University
Art Dept.
Atlanta GA 30303

Georgian College
School of Design and Visual Arts
1 Georgian Dr.
Barrie Ontario
CANADA L4M 3X9

Germantown Friends School
31 W. Coulter St.
Philadelphia PA 19144

Glassell School of Art
5101 Montrose
Houston TX 77006

Glenville State College
Dept. of Fine Arts
200 High St.
Glenville WV 26351

Golden West College
Visual Art Dept.
15744 Golden West St.
Huntington Beach CA 92647

Goshen College
Art Dept.
1700 S. Main St.
Goshen IN 46526

Grand Canyon University
Art Dept.
3300 W. Camelback Rd.
Phoenix AZ 85017

Grand Valley State University
Art and Design Dept.
147 CFAC
Allendale MI 49401

Grossmont College
Art Dept.
8800 Grossmont College Dr.
El Cajon CA 92020

Guilford Handcraft Center
P.O. Box 589
411 Church St.
Guilford CT 06437

Hamline University
Art Dept.
1556 Hewitt Ave.
St. Paul MN 55104

The Hand Workshop
1812 W. Main St.
Richmond VA 23220

Hands-On Glass
261 Baker St.
Corning NY 14830

Harbourfront Craft Studio
235 Queens Quay W.
Toronto Ontario
CANADA M5J 2G8

Harrisburg Area Community College
Division of Communication and Arts
3300 Cameron St.
Harrisburg PA 17110

Hartford Art School, University of Hartford
Art Dept.
200 Bloomfield Ave.
West Hartford CT 06117

Hartnell College
Visual Art Dept.
156 Homestead Ave.
Salinas CA 93901

Haystack Mountain School of Crafts
P.O. Box 518
Deer Isle ME 04627

Haywood Community College
Art Dept.
1 Freelander Dr.
Clyde NC 28731

Hazeltine School of Fine Jewelry
260 S. Lake, #174
Pasadena CA 91101

Heidelberg College
Art Dept.
Tiffin OH 44883

Highline Community College
Jewelry/Goldsmithing Program
P.O. Box 98000
Des Moines WA 98198

Hiram G. Andrews Center
727 Goucher St.
Johnstown PA 15905

Hofstra University
Art Dept.
107 Hofstra U
Hempstead NY 11550-1090

Holland School for Jewelers
P.O. Box 882
Selma AL 36702

Horizons Camp
108 N. Main St.
Sunderland MA 01375

Hui Noeau Visual Art Center
2841 Baldwin Ave.
Makawao HI 96768

Humboldt State University
Art Dept.
1 Harpst St.
Arcata CA 95521

Hutchinson Community Junior College
Art Dept.
600 E. 11th St.
Hutchinson KS 67501

Idaho State University
Art Dept.
P.O. Box 8291
Pocatello ID 83209

Illinois State University
Glass Art Dept.
Normal IL 61761

Indiana State University
Dept. of Art
Fine Arts 108
Terre Haute IN 47809

Indiana University of Pennsylvania
Art Dept.
115 Sprowls Hall
Indiana PA 15705

Indiana Wesleyan University
Art Dept.
4201 S. Washington
Marion IN 46953

Institute of American Indian Art
P.O. Box 20007
Sante Fe NM 87504

Inter American University of Puerto Rico
Call Box 5100
San German PR 00683

Interlochen Arts Academy
C Box 33, P.O. Box 199
Interlochen MI 49643-0199

International Gemological Institute
579 Fifth Ave., 7th Floor, #700
New York NY 10017

International Pacific College
Art Dept.
2 Annabel Ln., # 126
San Ramon CA 94583

Iowa State University
Art Dept.
288 College of Design
Ames IA 50011

Jacksonville University
Glass Art Dept.
2800 University Blvd N.
Jacksonville FL 32211

James Madison University
Art Dept.
Harrisonburg VA 22807

Jersey City State College
Art Dept.
2039 Kennedy Blvd.
Jersey City NJ 07304

Jewelry Arts Institute
2231 Broadway
New York NY 10024

Jewelry Design Institute
13354 Midlothian Tpk., #202
Midlothian VA 23113

Jody Serago's Shore Jewelry School
807 Bay Ave.
Somers Point NJ 08244

John Campbell Folk Art School
Rt. 1, Box 14A
Brasstown NC 28902

John Michael Kohler Arts Center
P.O. Box 489
Sheboygan WI 53082

Johnson County Community College
Visual Arts Program
12345 College Blvd.
Overland Park KS 66210-1299

Joliet Junior College
Art Dept.
1216 Houbolt Ave.
Joliet IL 60436-9352

Jonas & Associates Antique Jewelry and Gem
215 E. 80th St.
New York NY 10021-0531

Jones Junior College
Art Dept.
College Dr.
Ellisville MS 39437

Kalamazoo Institute of Arts
314 S. Park St.
Kalamazoo MI 49007-5102

Kansas State University
Dept. of Art
322 Willard Hall
Manhattan KS 66506

Kean College of NJ
Art Dept.
Union NJ 07083

Kendall College of Art and Design
Art Dept.
111 Division Ave. N.
Grand Rapids MI 49503-3194

Kent State University
School of Art
P.O. Box 5190
Kent OH 44242

Kentucky Folklife Program
P.O. Box H
Frankfort KY 40601

Kilgore College
Art Dept.
1100 Broadway
Kilgore TX 75601

Kutztown University of Pennsylvania
College of Visual and Performing Arts
Kutztown PA 19530

Lakeland Community College
Visual Arts Dept.
Rt. 306 at I90
Mentor OH 44060

Lane Community College
Art and Applied Design Dept.
4000 E. 30th Ave.
Eugene OR 97405

Laramie County Community College
Art Dept.
1400 E. College Dr.
Cheyenne WY 82007

Lawrence University
Art Dept.
Winston Art Center
Appleton WI 54911

Lewton-Brain Fontans Center
#300A 815 1st St. S.W.
Calgary Alberta
CANADA T2P 1N3

Liban, Felicia Enamel Studio
251-37 43rd Ave.
Little Neck NY 11363-1921

Linn Benton Community College
Fine and Applied Arts Dept.
6500 S.W. Pacific Blvd.
Albany OR 97321

Little House
800 Middle Ave.
Menlo Park CA 94025

Lock Haven University
Art Dept.
Lock Haven PA 17745

Long Beach City College, LAC Campus
Art Dept.
4901 E. Carson St.
Long Beach CA 90808

Long Island University, C.W. Post Campus
Art Dept.
720 Northern Blvd.
Greenvale NY 11548

Longwood College
Art Dept.
201 High St.
Farmville VA 23909

Louisiana State University
School of Art
123 Design Center
Baton Rouge LA 70803

Lourdes College
Art Dept.
6832 Convent Blvd.
Sylvania OH 43560

Loyola Marymount University
Art Dept.
Loyola Blvd. at W. 80th St
Los Angeles CA 90045

Loyola University of Chicago
Art Dept.
6525 N. Sheridan Rd.
Chicago IL 60626

Lubbock Christian University
Art Dept.
5601 W. 19th St.
Lubbock TX 79407-2099

Madison Area Technical College
Art Dept.
3550 Anderson St.
Madison WI 53704

Maine College of Art
Art Dept.
97 Spring St.
Portland ME 04101

Maine Photographic Workshops
Box 200, 2 Central St.
Rockport ME 04856

Mainline Center of the Arts
Old Buck Rd. and Lancaster Ave.
Haverford PA 19041

Manchester Institute of Art
148 Concord St.
Manchester NH 03104

Mankato State University
Art Dept.
Mankato MN 56002-8400

Mansfield University
Art Dept.
Allen Hall
Mansfield PA 16933

Maryland Institute College of Art
1300 Mount Royal Ave.
Baltimore MD 21217

Marywood College
Art Dept.
2300 Adams Ave.
Scranton PA 18509

Massachusetts College of Art
621 Huntington Ave.
Boston MA 02115

Memphis College of Art, Overton Park
1930 Poplar
Memphis TN 38104-2764

Mercyhurst College
Art Dept.
Glenwood Hills
Erie PA 16546

Mesa College
Dept. of Art/Continuing Education
P.O. Box 2647
Grand Junction CO 81502

Metal Arts Society of Southern California
1625 Electric Ave.
Venice CA 90291

Metropolitan State College
P.O. Box 173362
Arts Bldg., Box 59
Denver CO 80217-3362

Miami Jewelry Institute
The Bakehouse Art Complex
561 N.W. 32nd St.
Miami FL 33127

Miami University
Art Dept.
21 E. Collins St.
Oxford OH 45056

SCHOOLS/ART CENTERS

Michigan Hot Glass Workshop
29 W. Lawrence
Pontiac MI 48345

Middle Tennessee State University
Art Dept.
P.O. Box 25
Murfreesboro TN 37132-0001

Midland Art Council Studio School
180 W. St. Andrews
Midland MI 48640

Midland College
Fine Arts Dept.
3600 N. Garfield
Midland TX 79705

Midwestern State University
Division of the Arts
3411 Taft Blvd.
Wichita Falls TX 76308

Miles Community College
Art Dept.
2715 Dickinson St.
Miles City MT 59301

Millersville University
Art Dept.
Breidenstine Hall
Millersville PA 17551

Milwaukee Area Technical College
Jewelry Repair and Fabrication
700 W. State St.
Milwaukee WI 53233-1443

Milwaukee Technical College, South Campus
Art Dept.
6665 S. Howell Ave.
Oak Creek WI 53154

Minneapolis Technical College
Art Dept.
1415 Hennepin Ave. S.
Minneapolis MN 55403

Mission College
Art Dept.
3000 Mission College Blvd.
Santa Clara CA 95054

Missouri Southern State College
Art Dept.
3950 Newman Rd.
Joplin MO 64801

Mohave Comunity College, Kingman
Art Dept.
1971 Jagerson Ave.
Kingman AZ 86401

Monroe Community College
Art Dept.
1000 E. Henrietta Rd.
Rochester NY 14623-3105

Montana State University
School of Art
213 Haynes Hall
Bozeman MT 59717-0368

Monterey Peninsula College
Art Dept.
980 Fremont St.
Monterey CA 93940

Montgomery College
Art Dept.
51 Manakee St.
Rockville MD 20850

Moore College of Art and Design
20th and The Parkway
Philadelphia PA 19103

Moravian College
Art Dept.
1200 Main St.
Bethlehem PA 18018

Morningside College
Dept. of Art
1501 Morningside Ave.
Sioux City IA 51106

Mount Hood Community College
Art Dept.
26000 S.E. Stark St.
Gresham OR 97030

Munson-Williams-Proctor Institute
310 Genesee St.
Utica NY 13502

Murray State University
College of Fine Arts and Communication
Murray KY 42071

Natchitoches Technical Institute
Art Dept.
P.O. Box 657
Natchitoches LA 71458-0657

Nazareth College
Art Dept.
4245 East Ave.
Rochester NY 14618

Nebraska Wesleyan University
Art Dept.
5000 St. Paul Ave.
Lincoln NE 68504

New England Craft Program
108 N. Main St.
Sunderland MA 01375

New Mexico State University
Art Dept.
Box 3001, #3572
Las Cruces NM 88003

New Orleans Glass Workshop
2308 Tulane Ln.
New Orleans LA 70119

New Orleans School of Glass
727 Magazine St.
New Orleans LA 70130

New York Academy of Art
School of Figurative Art
111 Franklin St.
New York NY 10013

New York University
34 Stuyvesant St.
New York NY 10011

Norfolk State University
Fine Arts Dept.
Norfolk VA 23504

North Bennet Street School
39 N. Bennet St.
Boston MA 02113

Northeast School of Art and Design, Suffolk University
81 Arlington St.
Boston MA 02116

Northeast Wisconsin Technical College
Art Dept.
2740 W. Mason
Green Bay WI 54311

North Hennepin Community College
Art Dept.
7411 85th Ave. N.
Minneapolis MN 55445

North Seattle Community College
Art Dept.
9600 College Way N.
Seattle WA 98103

Northeastern Illinois University
Art Dept.
5500 N. St Louis
Chicago IL 60625

Northern Arizona University
Art Dept.
P.O. Box 6020
Flagstaff AZ 86011

Northern Illinois University
School of Art
DeKalb IL 60115-2854

Northwest Missouri State University
Art Dept.
800 University Dr.
Maryville MO 64468

Northwestern Michigan College
Art Dept.
1701 E. Front St.
Traverse City MI 49686

Nova Scotia College of Art and Design
5163 Duke St.
Halifax Nova Scotia
CANADA B3J 3J6

Ohio Northern University
Dept. of Art
500 S. Main St.
Ada OH 45810

Ohio State University
College of the Arts
1871 N. High St.
Columbus OH 43210

Ohio University
School of Art
Athens OH 45701

Ohio Wesleyan University
Dept. of Fine Arts
S. Sandusky St.
Delaware OH 43015

Oklahoma Baptist University
Art Dept.
500 W. University
Shawnee OK 74801

Oklahoma State University, Okmulgee
Jewelry Technology
1801 E. Fourth St.
Okmulgee OK 74447-3901

Oklahoma State University
Art Dept.
108 Bartlett Center for Studio Art
Stillwater OK 74078

Old Church Cultural Center
561 Piermont Rd.
Demarest NJ 07627

Old Dominion University
Art Dept.
Visual Arts Bldg.
Norfolk VA 23529

Olympic College
Art Dept.
1600 Chester Ave.
Bremerton WA 98337-1699

Orange Coast College
Division of Fine Arts
2701 Fairview Rd.
Costa Mesa CA 92628

Oregon School of Arts and Crafts
8245 S.W. Barns Rd.
Portland OR 97225

Oregon State University
Art Dept.
Memorial Union Craft Center East
Corvallis OR 97331

Otis College of Art and Design
Art Dept.
2401 Wilshire Blvd.
Los Angeles CA 90057

Pacific University in Oregon
Arts Division
2043 College Way
Forest Grove OR 97116

Paris Junior College, Texas Institute of Jewelry Technology
2400 Clarksville St.
Paris TX 75460

Parkland College
School of Fine and Applied Arts
2400 W. Bradley
Champaign IL 61821

Parsons School of Design
66 Fifth Ave.
New York NY 10011

Pasadena City College
Art Dept.
1570 E. Colorado Blvd.
Pasadena CA 91106

Penland School of Crafts
Penland Rd.
Penland NC 28765

Pennsylvania Academy of the Fine Arts
118 N. Broad St.
Phila PA 19102

Pennsylvania State University
School of Visual Arts
102 Visual Arts Bldg.
University Park PA 16802

Peters Valley Craft Center
19 Kuhn Rd.
Layton NJ 07851

Pilchuck Glass School (summer)
1201 316th St. N.W.
Stanwood WA 98292

Pilchuck Glass School (winter)
315 Second Ave. S., #200
Seattle WA 98104-2618

Pima Community College
Dept. of Art
2202 W. Anklam Rd.
Tucson AZ 85709-0295

Pittsburg State University
Art Dept.
1701 S. Broadway St.
Pittsburg KS 66762-7512

Pittsburgh Center for the Arts
1047 Shady Ave.
Pittsburgh PA 15232

Portland Community College
Art Dept.
12000 S.W. 49th St.
Portland OR 97219-0990

Pratt Institute
200 Willoughby Ave.
Brooklyn NY 11205

Pueblo Community College
Art Dept.
900 W. Orman
Pueblo CO 81004

Purdue University
Visual and Performing Arts
West Lafayette IN 47907-1352

R. Grey Company
818 W. Idaho St.
Boise ID 83702

Radford University
Art Dept.
P.O. Box 6965
Radford VA 24142

Rancho Santiago College
Art Dept.
1530 W. 17th St.
Santa Ana CA 92706

Revere Academy of Jewelry Arts
760 Market St, #900
San Francisco CA 94102

Rhode Island College
Art Dept.
600 Mount Pleasant
Providence RI 02908

Rhode Island School of Design
2 College St.
Providence RI 02903

Riverbend Art Center
1301 E. Siebenthaler Ave.
Dayton OH 45469

Rochester Community College
Art Dept.
Hwy. 14 E., 851 30th Ave., S.E.
Rochester MN 55904-4999

Rochester Institute of Technology
School for American Crafts
1 Lomb Memorial Dr.
Rochester NY 14623

Roger Williams University
Art Dept.
1 Old Ferry Rd.
Bristol RI 02809

Rowan College of NJ
Art Dept.
201 Mullicka Hill Rd.
Glassboro NJ 08028-1701

Sacramento City College
Art Dept.
3835 Freeport Blvd.
Sacramento CA 95882

Salem Art Association
600 Mission St. S.E.
Salem OR 97302

Salem State College
Art Dept.
352 Lafayette St.
Salem MA 01970

Sam Houston State University
Art Dept.
1028 21st St.
Huntsville TX 77341

San Diego Community College, Mesa
Fine Arts Dept.
7250 Mesa College Dr.
San Diego CA 92111

San Diego Community College, Point Loma
Art Dept.
3249 Fordham St.
San Diego CA 92110

San Diego State University
Art Dept.
5500 Campanile Dr.
San Diego CA 92182

San Jose State University
School of Art and Design
1 Washington Sq.
San Jose CA 95192

San Juan College
Art Dept.
4601 College Blvd.
Farmington NM 87402

Sangre De Cristo Arts Center
210 N. Santa Fe Ave.
Pueblo CO 81003

Santa Fe Glass Workshop
930 Baca St., #12
Santa Fe NM 87501

Santa Monica College
Art Dept.
1900 Pico Blvd.
Santa Monica CA 90405

SCHOOLS/ART CENTERS

Santa Rosa Junior College
Art Dept.
1501 Mendocino Ave.
Santa Rosa CA 95401

Savannah College of Art and Design
P.O. Box 3146
Savannah GA 31402-3146

Sawtooth Center for Visual Art
226 N. Marshall St.
Winston-Salem NC 27101

School of the Museum of Fine Arts
230 The Fenway
Boston MA 02115-9975

Scottsdale Community College
Art Dept.
9000 E. Chaparral Rd.
Scottsdale AZ 85250

Seattle Glassblowing Studio
2227 Fifth Ave.
Seattle WA 98121

Seattle Pacific University
Art Dept.
3 W. Cremona
Seattle WA 98119

Seton Hill College
Art Dept.
Greensburg PA 15601

Sharon Arts Center
RR 2, Box 361
Sharon NH 03458-9014

Shelbourne Craft School
Box 52
Shelbourne VT 05482

Silver Lake College
Art Dept.
2406 S. Alvernord
Manitowoc WI 54220

Skagit Valley College
Art Dept.
2405 College Way
Mount Vernon WA 98273-7564

Skidmore College
Art Dept.
Saratoga Springs NY 12866

Slippery Rock University of Pennsylvania
Art Dept.
Slippery Rock PA 16057

Smithsonian Resident Associates
Studio Arts Dept.
1100 Jefferson Dr. S.W., # 3077
Washington DC 20560

Snow College
Art Dept.
150 E. College
Ephraim UT 84627

Solano Community College
Art Dept.
4000 Suisun Valley Rd.
Suisun City CA 94585

Southampton College of Long Island
Division of Fine Arts
Southampton NY 11968

Southern Connecticut State University
Dept. of Art
501 Crescent St.
New Haven CT 06515

Southern Illinois University
School of Art and Design
Carbondale IL 62901-4301

Southwest Craft Center
300 Augusta
San Antonio TX 78205

Southwest Missouri State University
Art Dept.
901 S. National
Springfield MO 65804-0089

Southwestern Oklahoma State University
Art Dept.
100 Campus Dr.
Weatherford OK 73096

Southwest Texas State University
Art Dept.
San Marcos TX 78666

St. Norbert College
Division of Fine Arts
100 Grant St.
De Pere WI 54115

St Thomas Aquinas College
Dept. of Art
Rt. 340
Sparkhill NY 10976

St. Cloud State University
Visual Arts Dept.
720 Fourth Ave S.
St. Cloud MN 56301

St. Paul Technical College
Art Dept.
235 Marshall Ave.
St. Paul MN 55102

State University of New York, Brockport
Dept. of Art
Fine Arts Center
Brockport NY 14420

State University of New York, Buffalo
1300 Elmwood Ave.
Buffalo NY 14222

State University of New York, Geneseo
Dept. of Art
1 College Cir.
Geneseo NY 14454

State University of New York, New Paltz
Art Studio Dept.
75 S. Manheim Blvd.
New Paltz NY 12561-2499

State University of New York, Oswego
Art Dept.
125 Tyler Hall
Oswego NY 13126

Stephen F. Austin State University
Art Dept.
P.O. Box 13001 SFA
Nacogdoches TX 75962-3001

Stewart's International School for Jewelers
651 W. Indiantown Rd.
Jupiter FL 33458

Studio Jewelers
32 E. 31st St.
New York NY 10016

Sul Ross State University
Art Dept.
C-90
Alpine TX 79832

Syracuse University
Studio Arts
200 Crouse College, #202
Syracuse NY 13244-1010

Tacoma Community College
Art Dept.
6501 S. 19th St.,
Tacoma WA 98466

Taos Art School
Art Dept.
Box 2245
Ranchos De Taos NM 87557

Taos Institute of Arts
P.O. Box 2469
Taos NM 87571

Taylor University
Art Dept.
500 W. Reade Ave.
Upland IN 46989

Texas Tech University
Art Dept.
P.O. Box 42081
Lubbock TX 79409-2081

Texas Women's University
Art Dept.
P.O. Box 425469 TWU Station
Denton TX 76204

Thiel College
Art Dept.
75 College Ave.
Greenville PA 16125

Thundering Seas
P.O. Box 67
Depoe Bay OR 97341

Toledo Museum of Art
P.O. Box 1013
Toledo OH 43697

Torpedo Factory Art Center
105 N. Union St.
Alexandria VA 22314

Touchstone Center for Crafts
RD 1, Box 60
Farmington PA 15437

Towson State University
Art Dept.
Fine Arts Bldg.
Baltimore MD 21204-7097

Trenton State University
Art Dept.
Pennington Rd.
Trenton NJ 08650-4700

Trinity College of Vermont
Art Dept.
208 Colchester Ave.
Burlington VT 05401

Tulane University
Art Dept.
119 Newcomb Art Bldg.
New Orleans LA 70118

Tulsa Junior College
Art Dept.
909 S. Boston
Tulsa OK 74119

Tyler School of Art, Temple University
Beech and Penrose, #233
Elkins Park PA 19027

UCLA Extension
Art Dept.
10995 Le Conte Ave., Room 414
Los Angeles CA 90024-2883

University of Akron
School of Art
Folk Hall
Akron OH 44325-6030

University of Alaska
Art Dept.
#310 P.O. Box 755640
Fairbanks AK 99775-5640

University of Arizona
Art Dept.
P.O. Box 210002
Tucson AZ 85721-0002

University of Arkansas
Art Dept.
116 Fine Arts Bldg.
Fayetteville AR 72701

University of California, San Diego
Art Dept.
Craft Center 9500 Gilman Dr., #0338
La Jolla CA 92093

University of Central Oklahoma
Dept. of Visual Arts and Design
100 N. University Dr.
Edmond OK 73034-0180

University of Delaware
Art Dept.
103 Recitation Hall
Newark DE 19716

University of Florida
Art Dept.
P.O. Box 115801
Gainesville FL 32611

University of Georgia
Dodd School of Art
Jackson St.
Athens GA 30602-4102

University of Hawaii
Art Dept.
2535 The Mall
Honolulu HI 96822

University of Houston
Art Dept.
4800 Calhoun R.
Houston TX 77004-4893

University of Idaho
Art Dept.
Moscow ID 83844-2471

University of Illinois, Urbana-Champaign
School of Art and Design
408 E. PeabodyDr.
Champaign IL 61820

University of Iowa
School of Art
120 N. Riverside Dr.
Iowa City IA 52242

University of Kansas
School of Fine Arts
300 Art and Design Bldg.
Lawrence KS 66045-2261

University of Massachusetts, Dartmouth
College of Visual and Performing Arts
285 Old Westport Rd. N.
Dartmouth MA 02747

University of Michigan
School of Art
2000 Bonisteel Blvd.
Ann Arbor MI 48109-2136

University of Minnesota
Art Dept.
Minneapolis MN 55455

University of Minnesota, Duluth
Art Dept.
317 Humanities Bldg.
Duluth MN 55812

University of Missouri
Art Dept.
A126 Fine Arts Center
Columbia MO 65211

University of New Mexico
College of Fine Arts
Fine Arts Center, #1103
Albuquerque NM 87131-2039

University of New Orleans
Fine Arts Dept.
New Orleans LA 70148

University of North Carolina, Charlotte
Art Dept.
153 Rowe Arts Bldg.
Charlotte NC 28223

University of North Dakota
Art Dept.
P.O. Box 7099 University Station
Grand Forks ND 58202

University of North Texas
School of Visual Arts
P.O. Box 5098
Denton TX 76203

University of Northern Iowa
Art Dept.
Cedar Falls IA 50614-0362

University of Oklahoma
Art Dept.
520 Parrington Oval, #202
Norman OK 73034-0180

University of Oregon
Art Dept.
Eugene OR 97403

University of Pennsylvania
Art Dept.
34th and Spruce Sts.
Philadelphia PA 19104

University of Science and Arts of Oklahoma
Art Dept.
Chickasha OK 73018

University of South Carolina
Art Dept.
Sloan College
Columbia SC 29208

University of South Florida
Art Dept.
Division of Lifelong Learning
MGZ 144
Tampa FL 33620

University of Southwestern LA
Metal Art Dept
P.O. Box 43850 USL
Lafayette LA 70504

University of Texas, Arlington
Art Dept.
700 W. 2nd St.
Arlington TX 76109

University of Texas, Austin
Art Dept.
Austin TX 78712

University of Texas, El Paso
Art Dept.
El Paso TX 79968

University of Texas, Pan American
Art Dept.
1201 W. University Dr.
Edinburg TX 78539

University of the Arts
Broad and Pine Sts.
Philadelphia PA 19102

University of Toledo
Center for Visual Arts
620 Grove Pl.
Toledo OH 43620

University of Vermont
Art Dept.
304 Williams Hall
Burlington VT 05405

University of West Florida
Art Dept.
11000 University Pkwy.
Pensacola FL 32514-5751

University of Wisconsin
Art Dept.
6241 Humanities Bldg.
455 N. Park St.
Madison WI 53706

University of Wisconsin, Eau Claire
Art Dept.
Park and Garfield Aves.
Eau Claire WI 54701

SCHOOLS/ART CENTERS

University of Wisconsin, Green Bay
Division of Communication and the Arts
Green Bay WI 54701

University of Wisconsin, LaCrosse
Art Dept.
105 Center for the Arts
LaCrosse WI 54601

University of Wisconsin, Oshkosh
Art Dept.
Oshkosh WI 54901

University of Wisconsin, Parkside
Art Dept.
P.O. Box 2000
Kenosha WI 53141

University of Wisconsin, Platteville
Dept. of Fine Art
Art Bldg. # 212B
Platteville WI 53818

University of Wisconsin, River Falls
Art Dept.
River Falls WI 54022

University of Wisconsin, Stout
Dept. of Art and Design
Menomonie WI 54751

University of Wisconsin, Superior
Art Dept.
Superior WI 54880

University of Wisconsin, Whitewater
Art Dept.
800 W. Main St.
Center of the Arts 2073
Whitewater WI 53190

Utah State University
Art Dept.
W. Shynkaruk
Logan UT 84322-4000

Vermont Glass Workshop
Mackville Rd.
Hardwick VT 05843

Virginia Commonwealth University
School of the Arts
P.O. Box 842519
325 N. Harrison St.
Richmond VA 23284

Virginia State College
Fine Arts Dept.
Petersburg VA 23803

Wartburg College
Art Dept.
222 9th St. N.W.
Waverly IA 50677

Watershed
19 Brickhill Rd.
Newcastle ME 04553

Wayland Baptist University
Art Dept.
1900 W. Seventh
Plainview TX 79072

Wayne State University
Art Dept.
150 Community Arts
Detroit MI 48202

Weber State University
Art Dept.
Visual Arts
Odgen UT 84408-2001

Western Carolina University
Art Dept.
Belk Bldg.
Cullowhee NC 28723

Western Illinois University
Art. Dept.
32 Garwood Hall
Macomb IL 61455-1396

Western Montana College
Art Dept.
710 S. Atlantic
Dillon MT 59725

Western Oregon State College
Art Dept.
345 N. Monmouth Ave.
Monmouth OR 97361

Western State College of Colorado
Art and Technology Dept.
Quigley Hall
Gunnison CO 81231

**Westinghouse Vocational and
Technical High School**
Art Dept.
105 Johnson St.
Brooklyn NY 11201

William Jewell College
Art Dept.
500 College Hill
Liberty MO 64068

Wittenberg University
Art Dept.
P.O. Box 720
Springfield OH 45501

Wood Turning Center
P.O. Box 25706
Philadelphia PA 19144

Woodstock School of Art
Art Dept.
P.O. Box 338
Woodstock NY 12498

Worcester Center for Crafts
25 Sagamore Rd.
Worcester MA 01605

Xavier University of Louisiana
Art Dept.
7325 Palmetto
New Orleans LA 70125

YWCA, Craft Student League
610 Lexington Ave.
New York NY 10022

Yakima Valley Community College
Art Dept.
P.O. Box 1647
Yakima WA 98907

Yale University
Art Dept.
246 Church St.
New Haven CT 06520

Youngstown State University
Art Dept.
410 Wick Ave.
Youngstown OH 44555

RETAIL FAIRS/EXPOSITIONS

American Craft Enterprises
21 S. Eltings Corner Rd.
Highland NY 12528
800.836.3470

American Craft Marketing
P.O. Box 480
Slate Hill NY 10973-0480
914.355.2400

The American Folkways Festival
P.O. Box 334
Clintonville PA 16372

Americana Arts and Crafts Promotions
15 Cypress St.
Hagerstown MD 21742
301.791.2346

Annual Seafood and Arts Festival
Ruskin Chamber of Commerce
315 Tamiami Trail
Ruskin FL 33570
813.645.3808

Artisan Promotions, Inc.
83 Mount Vernon St.
Boston MA 02108
617.742.3973

Artrider Productions, Inc.
4 Deming St.
Woodstock NY 12498
914.679.7277

Arts in The Park
Arnot Art Museum
235 Lake St.
Elmira NY 14901-3191
607.734.3697

BRP Bill Riggins Promotions, Inc.
1403 W. Glen Ave.
Peoria IL 61614
309.69.CRAFT

Back to Grandma's Attic
P.O. Box 831670
Richardson TX 75083
214.238.9434

Baltimore's Festival of the Arts
21 S. Eutaw St.
Baltimore MD 21201

Banyan Arts and Crafts Festival
Coconut Grove Chamber of Commerce
2820 McFarlane Rd.
Coconut Grove FL 33133
305.558.1758

Central NY Village Artist and Craftsmen
P.O. Box 292
Hamilton NY 1334

Central Pennsylvania Festival of the Arts
P.O. Box 1023
State College PA 16804-1023

Cherry Creek Arts Festival
201 Fillmore St., #200
Denver CO 80206
303.355.2787

Classic Creations
P.O. Box 3644
Englewood CO 80155
800.967.6345

Classic Productions
927-C Mt. Eyre Rd.
Newtown PA 18940

Coconut Grove Arts Festival
P.O. Box 330757
Coconut Grove FL 33133
305.447.0410

Columbia Festival of the Arts
10221 Wincopin Cir., #100
Columbia MD 21044
410.715.3044

Columbus Arts Festival
55 E. State St.
Columbus OH 43215
614.224.2606

Connecticut Bridal Expo
Osborne/Jenks Productions
936 Silas Deane Hwy.
Weathersfield CT 06109
203.563.2111

Contemporary Crafts Market
1142 Auahi St., #2820
Honolulu HI 96814
213.936.1447

Cord Shows, Ltd.
4 Road K
Armonk NY 10504
914.273.4667

Country Folk Art Shows, Inc.
8393 E. Holly Rd.
Holly MI 48442
810.634.4151

Country Rose Florida Craft Shows
P.O. Box 1367
Stuart FL 34995
561.879.6035

Country at Heart Arts and Crafts Shows
P.O. Box 831670
Richardson TX 75083
214.783.1222

Countryside Arts and Crafts Shows
Events Management Group
P.O. Box 8845
Virginia Beach VA 23450
804.486.0220

Covered Bridge Festival of Parke County
RR 1, Box 168
Carbon IN 47837
317.344.9134

Crafts America
P.O. Box 603
Green Farms CT 06436
203.254.0486

Crafts Celebrations, Inc.
P.O. Box 625
Wayne PA 19087

Craft Producers
P.O. Box 300
Charlotte VT 05445
802.425.3399

Creative Faires
P.O. Box 1688
Westhampton Beach NY 11978

Fieldstone Shows, Inc.
6 Deerfield Dr.
Medfield MA 02052

Frederick Festival of the Arts
P.O. Box 3080
Frederick MD 21705

Great American Arts and Crafts
7818 64th Ln.
Glendale NY 11385
718.497.2873

Harvest Festival Fall Tour
A Division of Southex Exhibitions
601 N. McDowell Blvd.
Petaluma CA 94954
707.778.6300

High Country Craft Shows
High Country Art and Craft Guild
P.O. Box 2854
Asheville NC 28802
704.252.3880

Holiday Craft and Gift Show
P.O. Box 50096
Knoxville TN 37950
423.588.1233

Huff's Promotions, Inc.
4275 Fulton Rd. N.W.
Canton OH 44718
330.493.4130

International Art Resource
22191 Martella Ave.
Boca Raton FL 33433
407.451.4485

Jinx Harris Shows, Inc.
35 Pondview Dr.
Merrimack NH 03054
603.424.8014

Key Biscayne Art Festival
Rotary Club of Key Biscayne
P.O. Box 490174
Key Biscayne FL 33149
305.361.0049

Kutztown Fall Arts and Crafts Show
D & F Promotions
933 Rt. 25
Millersburg PA 17061
717.692.5628

Long's Park Art and Craft Festival
541 N. Mulberry St.
Lancaster PA 17603

M II Productions, Inc.
P.O. Box 938
Vernon CT 06066
860.745.5071

MAC Productions
705 Bugbee Ave.
Wausau WI 54401
715.675.6201

MD Craft and Folk Art Festival
P.O. Box 310
Cashtown PA 17310

Maitland Fine Arts Festival
The Rotary Club of Maitland Florida
P.O. Box 941234
Maitland FL 32794
407.263.5218

Manayunk Arts Festival
4320 Main St., #2
Philadelphia PA 19127
215.482.9565

Marketplace Potpourri
P.O. Box 831670
Richardson TX 75083
214.783.1222

Mountain Heritage Art and Crafts Festival
P.O. Box 426
Charles Town WV 25414

National Craft Fairs
National Crafts, Ltd.
4845 Rumler Rd.
Chambersburg PA 17201
717.369.4810

The Original Las Olas Art Festival
P.O. Box 2211
Fort Lauderdale FL 33303

Peters Valley Craft Fair
19 Kuhn Rd.
Layton NJ 07851

Philadelphia Craft Show
Philadelphia Museum of Art
P.O. Box 7646
Philadelphia PA 19101

Philadelphia Flower Show
Pennsylvania Horticultural Society
325 Walnut St.
Philadelphia PA 19106
215.625.8250

The Prom and Bridal Showcase
Dayton Hara Complex
1001 Shiloh Springs Rd.
Dayton OH 45415
513.278.4776

RETAIL FAIRS/EXPOSITIONS

Quail Hollow Events
P.O. Box 825
Woodstock NY 12494

Raab Enterprises
P.O. Box 33428
North Royalton OH 44133
216.237.3424

Rose Squared Productions, Inc.
12 Galaxy Ct.
Belle Mead NJ 08502

Saturday and Sunday in the Park with Art
The Cultural Council
7740 S.W. 142 St.
Miami FL 33158
305.238.0703

SOFA (Sculptural Objects/Functional Art)
210 W. Superior
Chicago IL 60610
800.563.SOFA

South Miami Art Festival
6410 S.W. 80th St.
South Miami FL 33143
305.661.1621

Southeast National Festival of Arts
SNFA Show Committee
1406 S. Missouri, #350
Clearwater FL 34616

Southern Lady Shows
P.O. Box 7719
Beaumont TX 77726
409.866.2725

Southex Exhibit Harvest Festivals
601 N. McDowell Blvd.
Petaluma CA 94954
707.778.6300

Springfield Bridal Expo
Osborne/Jenks Productions
936 Silas Deane Hwy.
Wethersfield CT 06109
203.563.2111

Steve Powers and Company
P.O. Box 2770
Fallsbrook CA 92088
619.731.9371

Sugarloaf Crafts Festival
200 Orchard Ridge Dr., #215
Gaithersburg MD 20878
800.210.9900

Thanksgiving Arts and Crafts Show
Crafts Etc. Etc. Etc., Inc.
Box 456
Dinwiddie VA 23841
804.469.3203

United Craft Enterprises
P.O. Box 326
Masonville NY 13804

United Productions
125 Fifth Ave. N.
Safety Harbor FL 34695
813.725.1562

Vermont Craft Workers, Inc.
P.O. Box 8139
Essex VT 05451
802.878.4786

Virginia Show Productions, Inc.
P.O. Box 305
Chase City VA 23924
804.372.3996

Washington Crafts Show
P.O. Box 603
Crafts America
Green Farms CT 06436
203.254.0486

Washington Square Outdoor Exhibits
115 E. Ninth St., #7C
New York NY 10003
212.982.6255

Washington Bridal Showcase
Showcase Productions
P.O. Box 2313
Fairfax VA 22031
703.425.1127

Waterfront Festivals
4 Greenleaf Woods Dr., #302
Portsmouth NH 03801
860.439.2021

Winter Park Sidewalk Festival
P.O. Box 597
Orlando FL 32790
407.671.6547

Woodwill Presents Art and Craft Expos
P.O. Box 5186
Hauppauge NY 11788
516.234.4183

WHOLESALE TRADE SHOWS

The Alternative Show
3724 Greenmount Ave.
Baltimore MD 21218
410.889.4745

American International Toy Fair
Toy Manufacturers of America
200 Fifth Ave.
New York NY 10010
212.675.1141

Americana Sampler, Inc.
103 Point East Dr.
Nashville TN 37216
615.227.2080

America's Mart/Atlanta
AMC, Inc.
240 Peachtree St. N.W., #2200
Atlanta GA 30303
404.220.2215

Apparel Mart
Suite 2 S. 345th
250 Spring St.
Atlanta GA 30303
404.220.2124

Atlantic Craft Trade Show
P.O. Box 519
Nova Nova Scotia
CANADA B3J 2R7
902.424.4212

Beckman's Handcrafted Gift Show
P.O. Box 27337
Los Angeles CA 90027-0337
213.962.5424

Buyers Market of American Craft
The Rosen Group
3000 Chestnut Ave., #300
Baltimore MD 21211
410.889.2933

California Gift Show
AMC, Inc.
240 Peachtree St. N.W., #2200
Atlanta GA 30303
404.220.2215

Canadian Gift and Tabletop Accessories Gift Show
265 Yorkland Blvd., #301
North York Ontario
CANADA M2J 1S5
800.750.1967

Chicago Gift Show
George Little Management
10 Bank St., #1200
White Plains NY 10606
914.421.3200

Dallas National Gift and Accessories Market
Dallas Market Center Company
2100 Stemmons Frwy.
Dallas TX 75207
800.521.0977

Denver Merchandise Mart Gift and Jewelry Show
451 E. 58th Ave.
Denver CO 80216-1422
303.292.6278

FAE Show
Ullo International, Inc.
40 Richards Ave.
Norwalk CT 06856
203.852.0500

FTD Association Convention and Trade Fair
29200 Northwestern Hwy.
Southfield MI 48034
810.355.6173

George Little Management
10 Bank St., #1200
White Plains NY 10606
914.421.3200

Goodrich and Company Promotions
P.O. Box 1577
Mechanicsburg PA 17055
717.796.2380

WHOLESALE TRADE SHOWS

International Contemporary Furniture Fair
George Little Management
10 Bank St., #1200
White Plains NY 10606
914.421.3200

International Craft Expo
Offinger Management Company
P.O. Box 2188
Zanesville OH 43702-2188
614.452.4541

International Fashion Boutique Show (IFBS)
The Larkin Group
P.O. Box 9103
Newton MA 02159
617.964.5100

International Home Furnishings Marketing Association
210 E. Commerce St.
High Point NC 27260-5238
910.888.3700

International Juvenile Products Show
Juvenile Products Manufacturers Association
236 Rt. 38 W., #100
Moorestown NJ 08057
609.231.8500

International Kids Fashion Show (IKFS)
The Larkin Group
P.O. Box 9103
Newton MA 02159
617.964.5100

JA International Jewelry Show
Blenheim Group
One Executive Dr.
Fort Lee NJ 07024
617.964.5100

Just Kidstuff
George Little Management
10 Bank St., #1200
White Plains NY 10606
914.421.3200

Landscape Industry Show
California Landscape Contractors Association
2021 North St., #300
Sacramento CA 95814
916.448.2522

Market Square
P.O. Box 899
Mechanicsburg PA 17055
717.245.9031

Merchandise Mart Properties, Inc.
470 The Merchandise Mart
Chicago IL 60654
312.527.7932

Miami Buyers Market of American Craft
The Rosen Group
3000 Chestnut Ave., #300
Baltimore MD 21211
410.889.2933

Mid-Atlantic Nurserymen's Trade Show
P.O. Box 314
Perry Hall MD 2128
410.882.5300

Montreal Hobby and Craft Show
PO Box 343, Stn. NDG
Montreal Quebec
CANADA H4A3P5
514.484.9414

The National Needlework Association
Offinger Management Company
P.O. Box 2188
Zanesville OH 43702
614.452.4541

National Stationery Show
George Little Management
10 Bank St., #1200
White Plains NY 10606
914.421.3200

Needlework and Accessories Trade Show
Needlework Markets, Inc.
415 Taberon Road
Peach Tree City GA 30269
404.631.1396

The New England Spring Flower Show
Massachusetts Horticultural Society
300 Massachusetts Ave.
Boston MA 02115
617.536.9280

New York Dollhouse and Miniature Trade Show
Offinger Management Company
P.O. Box 2188
Zanesville OH 43702
614.452.4541

The New York Flower Show
George Little Management
10 Bank St., #1200
White Plains NY 10606
914.421.3200

New York International Gift Fair
George Little Management
10 Bank St., #1200
White Plains NY 10606
914.421.3200

Philadelphia Buyers Market of American Craft
The Rosen Group
3000 Chestnut Ave., #300
Baltimore MD 21211
410.889.2933

Professional Crafters Trade Show
Offinger Management Company
P.O. Box 2188
Zanesville OH 43702-2188
614.452.4541

Rhode Island Spring Flower and Garden Show
George Little Management
10 Bank St., #1200
White Plains NY 10606
914.421.3200

San Francisco Furniture Show
Showplace Square Group
2 Henry Adams St., #450
San Francisco CA 94103
415.864.1500

Southern Nurserymen's Association
1000 Johnson Ferry Rd., #E130
Marietta GA 30068
404.973.9026

Two Rivers Art Expo
110 Glenview Dr.
Des Moines IA 50312
515.277.1511

Western Exhibitors
2181 Greenwich St.
San Francisco CA 94123
415.346.666

Woodworking Machinery and Furniture Supply Fair
Marketing Association Services
1516 S. Pontius Ave.
Los Angeles CA 90025

SHOPS/GALLERIES

A Mano Gallery
Martin and Ana Leyland
128 S. Main St.
New Hope PA 18938
215.862.5122

Abacus
Dana Heacock and Sal Scaglione
44 Exchange St.
Portland ME 04101
207.772.4880

Accents & Images
Joe and Diane Kreger
P.O. Box 402, Rt. 263
Peddler's Village
Lahaska PA 18931
215.794.7660

After the Rain
David Wallace
49 Mercer St.
New York NY 1001
212.925.6677

Alianza
Karen Rotenberg
154 Newbury St.
Boston MA 02116
617.262.2385

Allanstand Shop
Laurie Huttener
MP 382 Blue Ridge Pkwy.
Asheville NC 28815
704.298.7928

SHOPS/GALLERIES

The American Artisan
Nancy Saturn
4231 Harding Rd.
Nashville TN 37205
615.298.4691

American Crafts Gallery
Sylvia Ullman and Marilyn Bialosky
13010 Larchmere Blvd.
Cleveland OH 44120
216.231.2008

The American Hand
Susan Hirsch
125 Post Rd. E.
Westport CT 06880
203.226.8883

American Hand Plus
Ken Deavers
2906 M St. N.W.
Washington DC 20007
202.965.3273

An American Craftsman
Richard and Joanna Rothbard
317 Bleecker St.
New York NY 10012
212.727.0841

Animalia Gallery
Anita Tanner
403 Water St., P.O. Box 613
Saugatuck MI 49453
616.857.3227

Annie's
Ted and Kate Hocheiser
4 Dock Sq.
Rockport MA 01966
508.546.9125

Appalachian Spring
Paula and David Brooks
11877 Market St.
Reston VA 22046
703.478.2218

Art Fair Gallery
Bob Moore
332 W. Main St.
Brighton MI 48116
810.229.4060

The Artful Hand Gallery
Joseph and Mary Porcari
36 Copley Pl.
Boston MA 02116
617.262.9601

Artifax
Stephen and Patricia Swan
727 Hilltop
North Virginia Beach VA 23451
804.425.8224

Artique
Mike and Kathy Stutland
410 W. Vine St.
Civic Center Shops
Lexington KY 40507
606.233.1774

Artisans Crafts Mall
Julie Causey
4305 E. Hwy. 377
Granbury TX 76049
817.573.8083

Artisans Gallery
Helen Cuff
Box 133, Peddler's Village
Lahaska PA 18931
215.794.3112

Artisans Three
Helen S. Highley
Spring House Village Center, Box 550
Spring House PA 19477
215.643.4504

Arts & Artisans
Amy Hoffman
36 S. Wabash, #604
Chicago IL 60603
312.855.9220

Atypic Gallery
Deb and Denise Schmid
333 W. Brown Deer Rd.
Milwaukee WI 53217
414.351.0333

Balaman Gallery
Sema Balaman
1031 Lexington Ave.
New York NY 10021
212.472.8366

Brooke Pottery
Gloria Brooke
223 N. Kentucky Ave.
Lakeland FL 33801
941.688.6844

Cameron's
Danny Cameron
University Mall
Chapel Hill NC 27514
919.942.5554

Cedar Creek Gallery
Lisa Oakley
1150 Fleming Rd.
Creedmoor NC 27522
919.528.1041

Chiaroscuro
Peggy Wolf and Ronna Isaacs
700 N. Michigan Ave.
Chicago IL 60611
312.988.9253

Clarksville Pottery and Galleries
Syd and Arnold Popinsky
4001 N. Lamar Blvd., #200
Austin TX 78759
512.454.9079

The Clay Pot
Bob and Sally Silberberg
162 Seventh Ave.
Brooklyn NY 11215
718.788.6564

Common Wealth Gallery
Kathy and Rick Davidson
313 Fourth Ave.
Hyatt Regency
Louisville KY 40202
502.589.4747

The Company of Craftsmen
Jack Steele
43 W. Main St.
Mystic CT 06353
860.536.4189

Compliments Gallery
David and Jean Betses
P.O. Box 567-A
Kennebunkport ME 04046
207.967.2269

Compositions Gallery
Siegfred Ehrmann
317 Sutter St.
San Francisco CA 94108
415.693.9111

P. R. Coonley
Peg and John Coonley
10 South Rd.
Rockport MA 01966
508.546.6200

Cooper Street Craft Mall
Cathy Bleecker
1701 S. Cooper
Arlington TX 76010
800.653.1130

Cottage Crafters Craft Mall
4636 Broadway
Allentown PA 18104
610.366.9222

Country Friends Craft Mall
Jodi Moore and Ann Watson
117 N. Main
Eufaula OK 74432
918.689.7144

Countryside Craft Mall and Antiques
Linda Powers
35323 Plymouth Rd.
Livonia MI 48152
313.513.2577

Craft Company No. 6
Lynn Allinger and Gary Stam
785 University Ave.
Rochester NY 14607
716.473.3413

The Crafter's Gallery
Marta Shilling
2540 Barrow
Abilene TX 79605
915.695.3257

The Crafter's Market
114 Miln St.
Cranford NJ 07016
908.709.1200

Crafters Market of Minnesota Inc.
Ron Handevit
12500 Plaza Dr.
Even Prairie MN 55344
612.829.0830

Crafters Marketplace and Gifts
1403 W. Glen Ave.
Peoria IL 61614
309.692.7238

Crafters Mini Mall
Bill Ihrer
116 W. Tyler
Longview TX 75601
903.758.7713

Crafters Mini Mall
Bill Ihrer
235 S. Broadway
Tyler TX 75701
903.597.1290

Craftmaster's Mall
Barbara Peevey
1857 Briarcrest Dr.
Bryan TX 77802
409.776.0870

Crafts by Hand
Mona Housley
2802 Southwest Blvd.
San Angelo TX 76904
915.949.7611

The Craftsmen
Gloria Turk
Poughkeepsie Plaza Mall
South Poughkeepsie NY 12601
914.454.2336

Creative Hands
Rex and Debbie Rowland
22301 Eureka Rd.
Taylor MI 48180
313.287.9108

Davlins
Dave and Linda Looney
125 S.E. Main St.
Minneapolis MN
55414 612.378.1036

del Mano Galleries
Jan Peters and Ray Leier
11981 San Vicente Blvd.
Los Angeles CA 90049
310.476.8508

Dexterity
Shirley Zafirau
30 Church St.
Montclair NJ 07042
201.746.5370

Discoveries
Sally Fox Tennant
Columbia Mall
Little Patuxent Pkwy.
Columbia MD 21044
410.740.5800

Don Drumm Studios and Gallery
Don and Lisa Drumm
437 Crouse St.
Akron OH 44311
216.253.6268

Don Muller Gallery
Don Muller
40 Main St.
Northampton MA 01060
413.586.1119

Dusty Attic
Sharon Paul
3330 N. Galloway, #225
Mesquite TX 75150
214.613.5093

Dusty Attic
Jim Fuller and Donna Dulude
2853 Central Dr.
Bedford TX 76021
817.355.1375

Earthenworks
Cynthia and Donald Hoskins
713 First St.
LaConner WA 98251
360.466.4422

Edgecomb Potters
Richard Hilton
Rt. 27, Box 2104
Edgecomb ME 04556
207.882.6802

Elements
Claudia Gal and Ben Kettlewell
P.O. Box 1205, 338 Commercial St.
Provincetown MA 02657
508.487.4351

Eureka Crafts
Sarah Demrow-Dent
210 Walton St.
Syracuse NY 13202
315.471.4601

Fragile
Bob Brournon
175 M. Vernon Hwy.
Atlanta GA 30328
404.257.1323

Free Flight Gallery
Ed and Sandy Smith
9016 Bretshire
Dallas TX 75228
214.701.9566

Freehand
Carol Sauvion
8413 W. Third St.
Los Angeles CA 90048
213.655.2607

From Skilled Hands, Inc.
Linda Whapham
6401 Royalton Rd. N.
Royalton OH 44133
216.582.4520

Grande Olde Crafters Mall
Margaret Tankersville
2416 Music Valley Dr., #147
Nashville TN 37214
615.885.4147

The Grey Dove
Audrey Weinstock
1595 S. Livingston Ave.
Livingston NJ 07039
201.994.2266

Grovewood Gallery
Robert and Susan Levielle
111 Grovewood Rd.
Asheville NC 28804
704.253.7651

Hand of the Craftsman
Jan Haber
5 S. Broadway
Nyack NY 10960
914.358.6622

Hanson Galleries
Donna Milstein
800 W. Sam Houston Pkwy. N., #E118
Houston TX 77024
713.984.1242

Hearts & Crafts
Diane Mendel
Rt. 45 and Alliance Rd.
Woodbury Heights NJ 08097
609.384.8844

Hearts & Hands Craft and Antique Mall
Steve Ashmore
19300 Hwy. 59 N., #C
Humble TX 77338
800.653.1130

Homespun Crafters Mall
5110 W. Franklin Rd.
Boise ID 83705
208.336.2090

Homespun Crafters Mall
856 N.W. Bond St.
Bend OR 97701
541.383.3435

Homespun Treasures
Florence Farber
3650 Boston Rd., #Q
Lexington KY 40514
606.223.0851

Impulse Gallery
Frederick Bayer
188 Commercial St., P.O. Box 1375
Provincetown MA 02657
508.487.1154

Kentucky Art and Craft Gallery
Mary Ellen Hill
609 W. Main St.
Louisville KY 40202
502.589.0102

Knick Knacks
Kathy Jones
215 W. Camp Wisdom Rd., #8
Duncanville TX 75116
214.283.9007

Lakewood Craft Mall
Melissa Lopez
1908 Abrams Pkwy.
Dallas TX 75214
214.823.5799

SHOPS/GALLERIES

Langman Gallery
Richard Langman
2500 Moreland Rd.
Willow Grove Park, #1118
Willow Grove PA 19090
215.657.8333

Latitudes Gallery
Joan Castronuovo
4325 Main St.
Philadelphia PA 19127
215.482.0417

Linda's Arts & Crafts Emporium
Linda Cox
4808 Fairmont Pkwy., #304
Pasadena TX 77505
713.998.7879

Linda's Emporium II
Linda Cox
60 FM 1960
West Houston TX 77090
713.397.6061

Loop 281 Crafters Mall
Curtis Deshazer
1409D W. Loop 281
Longview TX 75604
903.295.9500

Mackerel Sky Gallery of Contemporary Craft
Tom and Linda Dufelmeier
217 Ann St.
East Lansing MI 48823
517.351.2211

The Magical Animal
Rosa and Marshall Weisfeld
3222 M St. N.W.
Washington DC 20007
202.337.4476

Mindscape Gallery
Ron Isaacson and Deborah Farber
1506 Sherman Ave.
Evanston IL 60201
847.864.2660

Nancy Margolis Gallery
Nancy Margolis
367 Fore St.
Portland ME 04101
207.775.3822

Nancy Markoe Fine American Crafts
Nancy Markoe
3112 Pass-a-Grille Way
St. Pete Beach FL 33706
813.360.0729

New Morning Gallery
John E. Cram
7 Boston Way
Asheville NC 28803
704.274.2831

Nostalgia Crafts & Antiques
Andy Jennings
128 Lakeland Plaza
Lewisville TX 75067
214.434.8004

Not Just Mud! Gallery
Lee and Lois Kupersmith
57 Bow St.
Portsmouth NH 03801
888.211.0311

Off the Wall
Theresa Bisceglia
616 Canyon Rd.
Santa Fe NM 87501
505.983.8337

Out of Hand
Karen Kline
6166 N. Scottsdale Rd., #502
Scottsdale AZ 85250
602.998.0977

Overwhelmed Gallery
Dennis and Emily Bergman
445 Plaza Real at Mizner Park
Boca Raton FL 33432
407.368.0078

Panache Gallery
Susan Cimionyotti
45104 Main St., P.O. Box 57
Mendocino CA 95460
707.937.1234

Pat's Art-A Brazos Craft Mall
103 S. University Parks Dr.
Waco TX 76706
817.756.3854

Peggy Sue's Crafts & Antiques
Peggy Sue Shepard
1034 W. University
Denton TX 76201
817.484.8852

Phoenix Rising Gallery
Maureen Pierre
2030 Western Ave.
Seattle WA 98121
206.728.2332

Pinch Pottery and the Ferrin Gallery
Leslie Ferrin, Mara Superior and Donald Clark
179 Main St.
Northampton MA 01060
413.586.4509

Pismo Contemporary Art Glass
Sandy Sardella
235 Fillmore St.
Denver CO 80206
303.333.2879

Plum Nelly Shop, Inc.
Joy Mullins and Jim Storey
1101 Hixson Pike
Chattanooga TN 37405
615.266.0585

Pratt's Antique and Craft Mall
1827 Troup Hwy.
Tyler TX 75701
903.531.9558

The Real Mother Goose
Stan and Judy Gillis
901 S.W. Yamhill
Portland OR 97205
503.223.9510

Riverdale Craft Mall
2516 Cantrell Rd., #J
Little Rock AR 72202
800.653.1130

Scott Laurent Galleries
Laurent J. Nicastro and Scott Alles
348 Park Ave. N.
Winter Park FL 32789
407.629.1488

The Seekers Collection and Gallery
Michael and Lynda Adelson
4090 Burton Dr.
Cambria CA 93428
805.927.4352

Seldom Seen
Don Gorenberg
820 E. Las Olas Blvd.
Ft. Lauderdale FL 33316
954.764.559?

Selo/Shevel Gallery
Elaine Selo and Cynthia Shevel
301 S. Main St.
Ann Arbor MI 48104
313.761.4620

Sheepscot River Pottery
Karen Kruger
Box 47, Rt. 1
Edgecomb ME 04556
207.882.9410

A Show of Hands
Hal Stevens
1665 W. Fifth Ave.
Columbus OH 43212
614.486.7119

Show of Hands
Deborah Kneale, Marcella Marsch, and Jim and Sharill Hawkins
2610 E. Third Ave.
Denver CO 80206
303.399.0201

Signature Stores Inc.
Arthur and Donna Grohe
Mashpee Commons, 10 Steeple St.
Mashpee MA 02649
508.539.0029

Skera Contemporary Crafts
Harriet and Stephen Rogers
221 Main St.
Northampton MA 01068
413.586.4560

Skillbeck Gallery
Cher Skillbeck
238 S. Sharon Amity Rd.
Charlotte NC 28211
704.366.8613

Society of Arts and Crafts
Beth Ann Gerstein
175 Newbury St.
Boston MA 02116
617.266.1810

Something Different
47 Main St.
Chester NJ 07930
908.879.8338

SHOPS/GALLERIES

Southern Creations Craft Mall
Donna Schroeppel
2853 Bartlett Blvd.
Memphis TN 38134
901.386.1010

Spectrum of America
Bob Libby
396 Old Kings Hwy.
Brewster MA 02631
509.385.3322

Studio 40, Inc.
Mary Chappell
The Greenbrier Hotel
White Sulphur Springs WV 24986
304.536.4898

Studio 41
George and Leah Perry Shelborne
739 First St., #41
Benicia CA 94510
707.745.0254

The Symmetree Company
Denis Berger
89 Church St.
Burlington VT 05401
802.658.1441

Symmetry
Gary and Dianne Zack
348 Broadway
Saratoga Springs NY 12866
518.584.5090

Tomlinson Craft Collection
Ginny Tomlinson
711 W. 40th St.
Baltimore MD 21211
410.338.1572

Topeo Gallery
Walter Hazzard
35 N. Main St.
New Hope PA 18938
215.862.2750

Unique Accents
Phyllis Gary and Andrew Fersten
3137 Dundee Rd.
Northbrook IL 60062
847.205.9400

A Unique Presence
Judy Harris and Ellen Royce
2121 N. Clybourn
Chicago IL 60614
312.929.4292

Upstreet Artes
Debbie Sigal
5878 1/2 Forbes Ave.
Pittsburgh PA 15217
412.521.8884

Whippoorwill Crafts
Bob and Karen Hohler
125 S. Market Bldg.
Boston MA 02109
617.523.5149

Wild Goose Chase
Irene Chang
1431 Beacon St.
Brookline MA 02146
617.738.8020

Zyzyx
Hazel Greenstein
1809 Reisterstown Rd.
Baltimore MD 21208
410.486.9785

PUBLICITY CONTACTS

ABC Directory of Arts and Crafts Events
P.O. Box 5388
Maryville TN 37802-5388
423.983.1374

Accent Magazine
485 Seventh Ave. #1400
New York NY 10018
212.594.0880

Accessories Magazine
P.O. Box 5550
Norwalk CT 06856
203.853.6015

Accessories Today
P.O. Box 2754
High Point NC 27261
910.605.0121

Accessory Merchandising
400 Knightsbridge Pkwy.
Lincolnshire IL 60069
800.621.2845

Ad Hoc Marketing
15 W. 72nd St.
New York NY 10023
212.947.6114

Adweek
1515 Broadway, 12th Floor
New York NY 10036
212.536.5336

American Artist Magazine
1515 Broadway
New York NY 10036
212.764.7300

American Ceramics Magazine
9 E. 45th St., #603
New York NY 10017-2403
212.309.6886

American Craft Magazine
72 Spring St.
New York NY 10012
212.274.0630

American Glass Review
P.O. Box 2147
Clifton NJ 07015
201.779.1600

American Jewelry Manufacturer
One State St., 6th Floor
Providence RI 02908
401.274.3840

American Way Magazine
American Airlines
4333 Amon Carter Blvd.
Fort Worth TX 76155
817.967.1804

American Woodworker Magazine
33 E. Minor St.
Emmaus PA 18098
610.967.8647

AmericanStyle Magazine
3000 Chestnut Ave., #304
Baltimore MD 21211
410.889.3093

Architectural Digest Magazine
6300 Wilshire Blvd., 11th Floor
Los Angeles CA 90048
213.965.3700

Art and Artifact Magazine
2451 Enterprise East Pkwy.
Twinsburg OH 44087
216.963.1011

Art and Auction Magazine
440 Park Ave. S., 14th Floor
New York NY 10016
212.447.9555

Art Business News
19 Old Kings Hwy. S.
Darien CT 06820
203.656.3402

Art Calendar Magazine
P.O. Box 199
Upper Fairmount MD 21867-0199
410.651.9150

Art Education Magazine
1916 Association Dr.
Reston VA 20091-1590
703.860.8000

Art New England Magazine
425 Washington St.
Brighton MA 02135
617.782.3008

Art News
48 W. 38th St.
New York NY 10018
212.398.1690

Artforum International Magazine
65 Bleecker St., 13th Floor
New York NY 10012
212.475.4000

The Artists' Magazine
1507 Dana Ave.
Cincinnati OH 45207
513.531.2222

PUBLICITY CONTACTS

Artweek
2149 Paragon Dr., #100
San Jose CA 95131-1312
408.441.7065

Atlanta Journal-Constitution
72 Marietta St.
Atlanta GA 30303
404.526.5151

Azure Magazine
2 Silver Ave.
Toronto Ontario
CANADA M6R 3A2

Baby Shop Magazine
4136 Library Rd., #200
Pittsburgh PA 15234
412.531.9742

Baltimore Magazine
16 S. Calvert St., #1000
Baltimore MD 21202
401.752.7375

Baltimore Sun
501 N. Calvert St.
Baltimore MD 21278
410.332.6000

Better Homes & Gardens Magazine
1716 Locust St.
Des Moines IA 50309-3023
515.284.3000

Black Enterprise Magazine
130 Fifth Ave.
New York NY 10111
800.727.7777

Blacksmith's Journal
P.O. Box 193
Washington MO 63090
314.239.7049

Boca Raton Magazine
6413 Congress Ave., #100
Boca Raton FL 33487
407.997.8683

Boston Magazine
300 Massachusetts Ave.
Boston MA 02115
617.262.9700

Bostonia
10 Lenox St.
Brookline MA 02146
617.353.3081

Bride's Magazine
360 Madison Ave.
New York NY 10017
212.880.2518

Butterick Make It! Magazine
161 Sixth Ave.
New York NY 10013
212.620.2500

Cable News Network
1 CNN Center, Box 105366
Atlanta GA 30348-5366
404.827.1500

Cape Cod Life
P.O. Box 1385
Pocasset MA 02559
508.564.4466

Casual Living Magazine
3301 Como Ave. S.E.
Minneapolis MN 55414
612.642.2913

Ceramic Arts and Crafts Magazine
30595 W. Eight Mile Rd.
Livonia MI 48152-1798
810.477.6650

Ceramics Monthly
P.O. Box 12448
Columbus OH 43212
614.488.8236

China, Glass and Tableware Magazine
P.O. Box 2147
Clifton NJ 07015
201.779.1600

Christian Science Monitor
One Norway St.
Boston, MA 02115
617.450.2312

Clay Times Magazine
P.O. Box 365
Waterford VA 22190
540.882.3576

Cleveland Plain Dealer
1801 Superior Ave.
Cleveland OH 44144
216.344.4500

Collector Editions Magazine
170 Fifth Ave.
New York NY 10010
212.989.8700

Collector's Mart Magazine
700 E. State St.
Iola WI 54990
715.445.2214

Collectors News
506 Second St.
Grundy Center IA 50638
319.824.6981

Colonial Homes Magazine
1790 Broadway, 14th Floor
New York NY 10019
212.830.2900

Colored Stone Magazine
60 Chestnut Ave., #201
Devon PA 19333-1312
610.293.1112

Commercial Appeal
495 Union Ave.
Memphis TN 38101
901.529.2211

Competitive Edge Magazine
National Home Furnishings Association
305 W. High St.
High Point NC 27260
800.621.9623

Consumers' Digest
5705 N. Lincoln Ave.
Chicago IL 60659
312.275.3590

Contemporary Doll Collector Magazine
30595 W. Eight Mile Rd.
Livonia MI 48152-1798
810.477.6650

Contract Design Magazine
One Penn Plaza
New York NY 10119
212.714.1300

Country Business Magazine
707 Kautz Rd.
St. Charles IL 60174
630.377.8000

Country Crafts Magazine
1716 Locust St.
Des Moines IA 50309
515.284.3000

Country Home Magazine
1716 Locust St.
Des Moines IA 50309
515.284.3000

Country Living Magazine
224 W. 57th St.
New York NY 10019
212.649.3500

Craft and Needlework Age
P.O. Box 420
Englishtown NJ 07726-0420
908.446.4900

Craft Arts International Magazine
P.O. Box 363
Neutral Bay Jct. Sydney
AUSTRALIA

Craft Digest
P.O. Box 155
New Britain CT 06050
203.225.8875

CraftNews
Ontario Crafts Council
35 McCaul St.
Toronto Ontario
CANADA M5T 1V7
416.977.3551

Craftmaster News
P.O. Box 39429
Downey CA 90239-0429
310.869.5882

Crafts Fair Guide
P.O. Box 5062
Mill Valley CA 94942

Crafts Magazine
P.O. Box 1790
Peoria IL 61656-1790
309.682.6626

Crafts Report
300 Water St.
P.O. Box 1992
Wilmington DE 19899
302.656.2209

PUBLICITY CONTACTS

Custom Woodworking Business
400 Knightsbridge Pkwy.
Lincolnshire IL 60069
708.634.4347

Decor Magazine
330 N. Fourth St.
St Louis MO 63102-2041
314.421.5445

Decorative Artists Workbook Magazine
1507 Dana Ave.
Cincinnati OH 45207
513.531.2690

Decorative Home Magazine
7 W. 34th St., 3rd Floor
New York NY 10001
212.630.4230

Denver Post
1560 Broadway
Denver CO 80202
303.820.1010

Design Times Magazine
1 Design Center Pl., #828
Boston MA 02210
617.443.0636

Designer Jewelry Showcase
8 W. 13th St.
New York NY 10011
212.989.0383

Early American Homes Magazine
6405 Flank Dr.
P.O. Box 8200
Harrisburg PA 17105
717.657.9555

Elle Decor Magazine
1633 Broadway, 44th Floor
New York NY 10019
212.767.5830

Entrepreneur Magazine
P.O. Box 57050
Irvine CA 92619-7050
714.261.2325

Essence Magazine
1500 Broadway, 6th Floor
New York NY 10036
212.642.0600

Exhibitor Magazine
206 S. Broadway, #745
Rochester MN 55904
507.289.6556

Family Business Magazine
229 S. 18th St.
Philadelphia PA 19103
215.790.7000

Family Circle Magazine
110 Fifth Ave.
New York NY 10011
212.463.1000

Fancy Food Magazine
20 N. Wacker Dr., #3230
Chicago IL 60606
312.849.2220

Fashion Accessories Magazine
65 W. Main St.
Bergenfield NJ 07621-1696
201.384.3336

The Fashion Newsletter
9700 Philadelphia Ct.
Lanham MD 20706-4405
301.731.5202

Festival Network Directory
19 Salem Rd.
Weaverville NC 28787
704.658.2779

Fiberarts Magazine
50 College St.
Asheville NC 28801
704.253.0467

Fine Woodworking Magazine
63 S. Main St.
Newtown CT 06470
203.426.8171

Floral Management
1601 Duke St.
Alexandria VA 22314-3406
703.836.8700

Florida Trend Magazine
P.O. Box 611
St. Petersburg FL 33731
813.821.5800

Florist Magazine
29200 Northwestern Hwy.
Southfield MI 48034
800.383.4383

Florists' Review
3641 S.W. Plass
Topeka KS 66611-2588
800.367.4708

Flowers and ... Magazine
12233 W. Olympic Blvd., #260
Los Angeles CA 90064
310.826.5253

Folk Art Magazine
61 W. 62nd St.
New York NY 10023
212.977.7170

Furniture Retailer Magazine
1301 Carolina St.
Greensboro NC 27401
919.378.6065

Furniture Today Magazine
P.O. Box 2754
High Point NC 27261
910.605.0121

Furniture World Magazine
530 Fifth Ave.
Pelham NY 10803
914.738.6744

Garden Design Magazine
100 Ave. of the Americas, 7th Floor
New York NY 10013
212.334.1212

Gift and Stationery Business Magazine
One Penn Plaza
New York NY 10119-0004
212.714.1300

Gifts and Decorative Accessories Magazine
51 Madison Ave.
New York NY 10010
212.689.4411

Giftware News Magazine
20 N. Wacker Dr., #3230
Chicago IL 60606
312.849.2220

Glass Art Magazine
P.O. Box 260377
Highlands Ranch CO 80163
303.791.8998

Glass Craftsman Magazine
P.O. Box 678
Richboro PA 18954
215.860.9947

Good Housekeeping Magazine
959 Eighth Ave.
New York NY 10019
212.649.2200

The Guild Sourcebook
931 E. Main St., #106
Madison WI 53703
800.969.1556

Hands On Guide
255 Cranston Crest
Escondido CA 92025-7037
619.747.8206

Handwoven Magazine
201 E. Fourth St.
Loveland CO 80537
303.669.7672

The Harris List
P.O. Box 142
La Veta CO 81055
719.742.3146

Haut Decor Magazine
P.O. Box 371369
Miami FL 33137-3650
305.576.1677

Hearth and Home Magazine
P.O. Box 2008
Laconia NH 03247
603.528.4285

Home Accents Today Magazine
7025 Albert Pick Rd.
Greensboro NC 27409-0519
919.605.1112

Home Furniture Magazine
63 S. Main St.
Newtown CT 06470
203.426.8171

Home Magazine
1633 Broadway, 44th Floor
New York NY 10019
212.767.6000

PUBLICITY CONTACTS

Home Textiles Today Magazine
245 W. 17th St.
New York NY 10011-5300
212.337.6900

Hospitality Design Magazine
355 Park Ave. S., 4th Floor
New York NY 10010
212.592.6330

House Beautiful Magazine
1700 Broadway, 29th Floor
New York NY 10019
212.903.5084

Ideas Magazine
P.O. Box 343392
Coral Gables FL 33114
305.238.0557

Interior Decorators' Handbook
342 Madison Ave., #1901
New York NY 10173-0002
212.661.1516

Interior Design Magazine
245 W. 17th St.
New York NY 10016
212.645.0067

Interiors and Sources Magazine
450 Skokie Blvd., #507
Northbrook IL 60062
708.498.9880

Interiors Magazine
1515 Broadway, 11th Floor
New York NY 10036
212.536.5141

Jewelers Inc. Magazine
P.O. Box 42
Rochford SD 57778-0042
605.584.2505

Jewelers' Circular-Keystone Magazine
One Chilton Way
Radnor PA 19089
610.964.4474

Jewelry Newsletter International
2600 S. Gessner Rd.
Houston TX 77063
713.783.0100

Jewish Times
2104 N. Charles St.
Baltimore MD 21218
410.752.3504

Juvenile Merchandising
2125 Center Ave., #305
Fort Lee NJ 07024-5859
201.592.7007

LDB Interior Textiles Magazine
342 Madison Ave., #1901
New York NY 10173
212.661.1516

Ladies' Home Journal Magazine
125 Park Ave.
New York NY 10017
212.557.6600

Lady's Circle Patchwork Quilts
28 W. 25th St.
New York NY 10010
212. 647.0222

Landscape Architecture Magazine
4401 Connecticut Ave. N.W., 5th Floor
Washington DC 20008-2302
202.686.2752

Lapidary Journal Magazine
60 Chestnut Ave., #201
Devon PA 19333
215.293.1112

Lifetime Television - Our Home
309 W. 49th St.
New York NY 10019
212.424.7000

Martha Stewart Living Magazine
11 W. 43rd St., 24th Floor
New York NY 10036
212.522.7800

McCall's Magazine
110 Fifth Ave.
New York NY 10011
212.463.1000

Media Distribution Service (MDS)
307 W. 36th St.
New York NY 10018
212.279.4800

Metalsmith Magazine
5009 Londonderry Dr.
Tampa FL 33647
813.977.5326

Metropolis Magazine
177 E. 87th St.
New York NY 10028
212.722.5050

Metropolitan Home Magazine
1633 Broadway, 41st Floor
New York NY 10019-6708
212.767.6041

Miami Herald
1 Herald Plaza
Miami FL 33132

Mid-Atlantic Country
250 S. President St., #1
Baltimore MD 21202-4422
410.539.0005

Mid-Atlantic Craft Show List
P.O. Box 161
Catasauqua PA 18032-0161
610.264.5325

Mid-Atlantic Events Magazine
1080 N. Delaware Ave.
Philadelphia PA 19125-4330
800.521.8588

Midwest Living Magazine
1912 Grand Ave.
Des Moines IA 50309
515.284.2662

Minority Business News
11333 N. Central Expwy., #201
Dallas TX 75243
214.606.3986

Mirabella Magazine
1633 Broadway, 44th Floor
New York NY 10019
212.767.5800

Modern Bride Magazine
249 W. 17th St., 2nd Floor
New York NY 10011
212.462.3300

Modern Jeweler Magazine
445 Broad Hollow Rd., #21
Mellville NY 11747
516.845.2700

Modern Maturity Magazine
3200 E. Carson St.
Lakewood CA 90712
310.496.2277

Modern Woodworking
P.O. Box 640
Collierville TN 38037901.853.7470

Nation's Business Magazine
1615 H St. N.W.
Washington DC 20062-2000
202.463.5650

National Business Woman
2012 Massachusetts Ave. N.W.
Washington DC 20036
202.293.1100

National Hardwood Magazine
1235 Sycamore View
Memphis TN 38134
901.372.8280

National Jeweler Magazine
One Penn Plaza, 11th Floor
New York NY 10119
212.615.2380

Native Arts Circle
1433 E. Franklin Ave.
Minneapolis MN 55404
612.870.7173

New Mexico Magazine
1100 Joseph Montoya Bldg.
Santa Fe NM 87501
505.827.7447

New Woman Magazine
215 Lexington Ave.
New York NY 10016-5675
212.251.1500

New York Daily News
450 W. 33rd St.
New York NY 10011
212.210.2100

New York Post
1211 Ave. of the Americas
New York NY 10036
212.930.8000

New Yorker Magazine
25 W. 43rd St., 17th Floor
New York NY 10036
212.536.5400

NICHE Magazine
3000 Chestnut Ave., #304
Baltimore MD 21211
410.889.3093

PUBLICITY CONTACTS

North Carolina Magazine
P.O. Box 2508
Raleigh NC 27602
919.836.1400

Northern California Home and Garden
618 Santa Cruz Ave.
Menlo Park CA 94025
415.324.1818

Ontario Craft Magazine
Ontario Crafts Council
35 McCaul St.
Toronto Ontario
CANADA M5T 1V7
416.977.3551

Ornament Magazine
P.O. Box 2349
San Marcos CA 92079
619.599.0222

Parents Magazine
685 Third Ave.
New York NY 10017
212.878.8700

Party and Paper Retailer Magazine
70 New Canaan Ave.
Norwalk CT 06850-2600
203.845.8020

Pennsylvania Magazine
P.O. Box 576
Camp Hill PA 17011-0576
717.697-4660

People Magazine
Time & Life Bldg.
Rockefeller Center
New York NY 10020
212.522.1212

Philadelphia Business Journal
400 Market St., #300
Philadelphia PA 19106
215.238.1450

Philadelphia Magazine
1818 Market St.
Philadelphia PA 19103
215.564.7700

Pittsburgh Post-Gazette
34 Boulevard of the Allies
Pittsburgh PA 15222
412.263.1100

Popular Ceramics Magazine
N7450 Aanstad Rd.
Iola WI 54945
715.445.5000

Popular Woodworking
1507 Dana Ave.
Cincinnati OH 45207
513.531.2690

Preservation Magazine
1785 Massachusetts Ave. N.W.
Washington DC 20016
202.588.6072

Professional Craft Journal
P.O. Box 1063
Pala Alto CA 94302
415.324.4156

Professional Quilter Magazine
104 Bramblewood Ln.
Lewisberry PA 17339-9535
717.691.8176

Public Broadcasting Service
1320 Braddock Pl.
Alexandria VA 22314
703.739.5000

Quilt Magazine
1115 Broadway, 8th Floor
New York NY 10010
212.807.7100

Redbook Magazine
224 W. 57th St.
New York NY 10019
212.649.3450

Retail Ideas Magazine
P.O. Box 2754
High Point NC 27261
910.605.0121

Rocky Mountain News
400 W. Colfax Ave.
Denver CO 80204
303.892.5000

Romantic Homes Magazine
707 Kautz Rd.
St. Charles IL 60174
630.377.8000

Ronay Guide to Shows
2950 Pangborn Rd.
Decatur GA 30033
770.939.2452

Rosen Publishing
3000 Chestnut Ave.. #304
Baltimore MD 21211
410.889.3093

Sarasota Herald Tribune
801 S. Tamiami Trail
Sarasota FL 34236
813.953.7755

Shuttle, Spindle and Dyepot Magazine
3327 Duluth Hwy.
Duluth GA 30136
770.495.7702

Small Businesss Opportunities
1115 Broadway, 8th Floor
New York NY 10010

Small World Magazine
225 W. 34th St.
New York NY 10001
212.563.2742

South Florida Business Journal
1050 Lee Wagener Blvd., #302
Ft Lauderdale FL 33315
305.359.2109

South Florida Magazine
P.O. Box 019068
Miami FL 33101
305.445.4500

Southern Accents Magazine
2100 Lakeshore Dr.
Birmingham AL 35202
205.877.6000

Southern Living Magazine
2100 Lakeshore Dr.
Birmingham AL 35209
205.877.6000

Southwest Art Magazine
5444 Westheimer, #1440
Houston TX 77056
713.850.0990

Souvenirs and Novelties
7000 Terminal Sq., #210
Upper Darby PA 19082-2310
215.734.2420

Stained Glass Magazine
6 S.W. Second St., #7
Lee's Summit MO 64063
816.524.9313

Stained Glass News
4060 29th St. S.E.
Grand Rapids MI 49512
616.942.1182

Stores Magazine
325 Seventh St. N.W.
Washington DC 20004
202.626.8101

Sumner Communications
24 Grassy Plain St.
Bethel CT 06801
203.748.2050

Sunset Magazine
80 Willow Rd.
Menlo Park CA 94025
415.321.3600

Sunshine Artist Magazine
2600 Temple Dr.
Winter Park FL 32789
800.597.2573

Surface Design Journal
P.O. Box 20799
Oakland CA 94620-0799
707.829.3110

Threads Magazine
63 S. Main St., Box 355
Newtown CT 06470
203.426.8171

Today Show/ NBC News WRCT-TV
Willard Scott
4001 Nebraska Ave. N.W.
Washington DC 20016
202.885.4000

Today's Woodworker
4365 Willow Dr.
Medina MN 55340
612.478.8232

Toledo Blade
541 Superior St.
Toledo OH 43660
419.245.6000

PUBLICITY CONTACTS

Toronto Life Magazine
59 Front St. E.
Toronto Ontario
CANADA M5E 1B3
416.364.3333

Town and Country Magazine
1700 Broadway, 30th Floor
New York NY 10019-5905
212.903.5000

Tradeshow Week
5700 Wilshire Blvd., #120
Los Angeles CA 90036
213.965.5300

Traditional Home Magazine
1716 Locust St.
Des Moines IA 50309
515.284.3000

USA Today
1000 Wilson Blvd.
Arlington VA 22229
703.276.3400

USAir Magazine
122 E. 42nd St.
New York NY 10168
212.499.3550

Veranda Magazine
455 E. Paces Ferry Rd. N.E., #216
Atlanta GA 30305-2504
404.261.3603

Victoria Magazine
224 W. 57th St.
New York NY 10019
212.649.3706

Visual Merchandising and Store Design Magazine
407 Gilbert Ave.
Cincinnati OH 45202-2285
513.421.2050

W Magazine
7 W. 34th St., 3rd Floor
New York NY 10001
212.630.4000

Washington Business Journal
2000 14th St. N., # 500
Arlington VA 22201
703.875.2200

Washingtonian Magazine
1828 L St. N.W., #200
Washington DC 20036
202.296.3600

Watch and Clock Review Magazine
2403 Champa
Denver CO 80205
303.296.1600

West Art Magazine
P.O. Box 6868
Auburn CA 95604
916.885.0969

Woman's Day Home Decorating Ideas
1633 Broadway, 42nd Floor
New York NY 10019-6708
212.767.6000

Woman's Day Magazine
1633 Broadway, 42nd Floor
New York NY 10019
212.767.6000

Woman's World Magazine
270 Sylvan Ave.
Englewood Cliffs NJ 07632
201.569.6699

Women's Wear Daily
7 W. 34th St., 3rd Floor
New York NY 10001
212.630.3500

Wood and Wood Products Magazine
4000 Knightsbridge Pkwy.
Lincolnshire IL 60069
847.634.4347

Wood Digest
1233 Janesville Ave.
Fort Atkinson WI 53538
414.563.6388

Wood Magazine
1912 Grand Ave.
Des Moines IA 50309-3379
515.284.2235

Wood Strokes and Weekend Woodcrafts
1041 Shary Circle
Concord CA 94518
510.671.9852

Woodsmith Magazine
2200 Grand Ave.
Des Moines IA 50312-5340

Woodwork Magazine
42 Digital Dr., #5
Novato CA 94949
415.382.0580

Working Woman TV Show
Albritton Productions
3007 Tilden St. N.W.
Washington DC 20008
202.364.6820

Working from Home
Business News Network
5025 Centennial Blvd.
Colorado Springs CO 80919
719-528.7040

Yankee Magazine
P.O. Box 520
Dublin NH 03444
603.563.8111

Your Company Magazine
Time & Life Bldg.
Rockefeller Center
New York NY 10020
212.522.1212

BOOKS & VIDEO

Titles published by Chilton Book Company are available from Krause Publications, 700 East State Street, Iola, WI 54990-0001. Add $3.25 shipping and handling for the first book ordered and $2.00 for each additional. Or call 888.457.2873 and use your VISA, Mastercard, American Express or Discover card to order. (Wisconsin residents add 5.5% sales tax; Illinois residents add 7.5% sales tax.)

The Art of Manipulating Fabric
by Colette Wolff
This book categorizes all major dimensional techniques and gives examples of variations both traditional and modern. The result is an encyclopedia of techniques that resurface, reshape, restructure, and reconstruct fabric.
320 pp, illustrated throughout, $29.95

Embellishments
Adding Glamour to Garments
by Linda Fry Kenzle
An idea book that explains wearable art with appliqué, patchwork, beading, ribbon, lace, fringe, frogs, braids, passementerie, and epaulets.

Dozens of techniques with illustrations for enhancing fabric, garments, and accessories.
176 pp + 8 color pp, $18.95

Hold It!
How to Sew Bags, Totes, Duffels, Pouches, & More
by Nancy Restuccia
Instructions for flat bags, tote bags, cases, rolls, and pouches. Each of the 22 basic projects includes a difficulty rating, illustrated step-by-step instructions, and a list of variations.
144 pp + 8 color pp, $17.95

The New Work of Our Hands
Contemporary Jewish Needlework and Quilts
by Mae Rockland Tupa
Ideas, inspirations, and patterns for samplers, wedding canopies, hallah covers, banners, and other items for family and holiday celebrations. Filled with drawings, photos, and descriptions of featured works by the author and noted craftspeople.
160 pp + 16 color pp, $19.95

The Vest Book
by Jacqueline Farrell
Twenty original and exciting projects with complete step-by-step instructions show how easy it is to make a vest or transform an old one. Each of the stunning garments conveys a unique fashion expression, using a different craft or needlework technique: peruvian appliqué, buttons and braids, floral embroidery, stencil, and much more!
128 pp, color throughout, $$19.95

The Art and Craft of Paper Sculpture
A Step-by-Step Guide to Creating 20 Outstanding and Original Paper Projects
by Paul Jackson
Twenty projects, ranging from framed relief pictures to freestanding three-dimensional objects and mobiles. Includes step-by-step instructions, illustrated by full-color photography and templates.
128 pp, color throughout, $19.95

Beautiful Beads
by Alexandra Kidd
Easy-to-follow instructions for creating more than 50 projects, including: jewelry, embellishments for your wardrobe, and accents for home decor. Techniques range from the basics of stringing to loomwork and bead embroidery.
128 pages, color throughout, $19.95

Contemporary Decoupage
Fresh Ideas for Gifts, Keepsakes, and Home Furnishings
by Linda Barker
Over 35 innovative projects for the home, including chairs, boxes, cabinets, vases, lampshades, picture frames, decorative bowls, and more. Complete instructions illustrated by step-by-step color photographs with expert advice on techniques and equipment. Six sheets of ready-to-photocopy decoupage motifs are included.
112 pp, color throughout, $19.95

Craft an Elegant Wedding
by Naomi Baker and Tammy Young
For the bride and bridegroom, their families and friends, this is the first-ever book to help plan events and craft the items to make each occasion unique, from the engagement party through showers and the rehearsal dinner, to the wedding and reception. Make over 30 easy projects.
144 pp + 8 color pp, $17.95

Crafting as a Business
by Wendy Rosen
Provides the crafts artisan with a blueprint for success in starting a business in crafts—from drafting a sound business plan, to the day-to-day management challenges of regulating production and keeping accounts. This book provides all the guideposts any serious craftsperson will need to navigate the way to success in business.
160 pp, two-color throughout, $19.95

Exotic Beads
by Sara Withers
Learn how to make sophisticated, professional-looking jewelry—necklaces, chokers, earrings and bracelets—with readily available materials. Projects range from simple ideas for beginners to intricate and inspirational ideas for more experienced bead workers. Basic techniques and clearly annotated color photography show how to create 45 distinctive designs easily.
128 pp, color throughout, $19.95

Fanciful Frames
by Juliet Bawden
Starting with the basics of making and decorating simple frames, the author explores some of the thousands of different ways to create beautiful, functional surrounds for photographs, paintings, prints, or mirrors. 50 easy-to-follow projects, with step-by-step photos. Includes many craft techniques, all kinds of materials, and embellishments to existing frames.
160 pp, color throughout, $19.95

Glorious Greetings
Creating One-of-a-Kind Cards
by Kate Twelvetrees
An exciting and inspiring guide to making beautiful, unique greeting cards that are destined to become treasured keepsakes. Crafters of all skill levels will enjoy making the 100 card projects included, each accompanied by illustrated step-by-step instructions and full-color photographs. A wide range of techniques are used, from quilting to collage, from paper casting to stamping, from patchwork to stenciling.
128 pp, color throughout, $19.95

The Irresistible Bead
Designing and Creating Exquisite Beadwork Jewelry
by Linda Fry Kenzle
This book includes 20 exciting jewelry projects, each explained step by step with color illustrations and photographs. Designs include elegant Victorian brooches, shimmering amulet bags, and brightly colored clay necklaces. Chapters on Wire Work, Polymer Clay, Beading on a Ground, Weaving Beads, Stringing Beads, and Designing Your Own Jewelry.
128 pp, color throughout, $19.95

Papier Mâché Style
by Alex MacCormick
Contains 100 step-by-step directions and recipes for attractive and imaginative objects that will inspire beginners and skilled craftspeople alike. Projects range from jewelry, bowls, vases to mirrors, shelves, and dolls.
128 pp, color throughout, $15.95

Silk Flowers
by Judith Blacklock
Create lovely and lasting floral designs to exactly complement any decor. Introduces types and colors; teaches texture, balance, dominance, contrast, and movement; covers containers and accessories. Lovely four-color diagrams and inspiring photographs throughout.
160 pp, color throughout, $19.95

StampCraft
Dozens of Creative Ideas for Stamping on Cards, Clothing, Furniture, and More
by Cari Haysom
Tremendously versatile, stamping can be used on a very small scale to create personalized cards and stationery, or on a very large scale to transform walls, drapes, and furniture for a unique, custom look. Over 40 projects with clear step-by-step instructions and illustrated throughout with color photographs.
128 pp, color throughout, $19.95

Stamping Made Easy
by Nancy Ward
Creating original designs with "rubber" stamps is one of the hottest crafting trends today. Shows the various stamps available (rubber, polymer, magnetized, roller, etc.), then presents a wide variety of stamping techniques and projects.
113 pp + 8 color pp, $16.95

Textile Artistry
edited by Valerie Campbell-Harding
With the help of step-by-step diagrams, instructions, and color photographs, readers will learn to make: ribbon and fabric floral bags, satin-stitched flower pots, a quilted jacket, a felt wall-hanging and more. Projects incorporate fabric painting and quilting as well as hand and machine embroidery.
128 pp, color throughout, $17.95

Timeless Bouquets
Decorate and Design with Dried Flowers
by Mireille Farjon
Designed to make professional-looking dried flower arrangements a snap. Part One tells you how to choose and buy flowers, or pick and dry them yourself. Part Two shows you how to achieve a particular look or style, with dozens of gorgeous arrangements in situ, all photographed in vivid color.
128 pp, color throughout, $18.95

Electric Kiln Ceramics
A Guide to Clays and Glazes, 2nd Edition
by Richard Zakin
This guide will allow potters to use the electric kiln to achieve clear, brilliant colors and richly textured surfaces. Completely revised glaze recipes and updated health and safety information. Photography featuring the work of artists from around the world.
304 pp + 16 color pp, $39.95

Hand-Formed Ceramics
Creating Form and Surface
by Richard Zakin
Presents potters with a global survey of various artists' techniques for creating sculpture, vessels, and wall pieces. Instructions, advantages, and disadvantages of forming methods are discussed, plus tips on combining forming methods. Includes 300 black-and-white photos and 16 pages of color.
244 pp + 16 color pp, $39.95

The Potter's Palette
A Practical Guide to Creating Over 700 Illustrated Glaze and Slip Colors
by Christine Constant and Steve Ogden
Potters struggle constantly with the uncertainty and frustration of mixing one color—and getting an entirely different fired result. This reference guide to glaze calculation, formulation, and use is the answer to a serious need. Also includes color bars to show actual fired results, and simple calculations so the potter may make adjustments for the type and length of firing time.
80 pp, color throughout, $19.95

The Design and Creation of Jewelry
3rd Edition
by Robert von Neumann
A standard reference for craftspeople, professional jewelry designers, and students of jewelry making.
320 pp + 12 color pp, $19.95

How to Work in Stained Glass (Second Edition)
by Anita and Seymour Isenberg
The premier source of basic information.
336 pp + 20 color pp, $19.95

Modeling in Wax for Jewelry and Sculpture
by Lawrence Kallenberg
The text for all phases of wax casting and mold-making.
252 pp + 8 color pp, $32.95

BOOKS & VIDEO

Silversmithing
by Rupert Finegold and William Seitz
The basics of smithing, types and properties of metals, tools, and techniques.
480 pp, $39.95

Mail Order...Starting Up, Making It Pay
by J. Frank Brumbaugh
In this step-by-step guide, you learn what a customer looks for in a product, how to choose a product or service that sells, how much to charge, how to prepare sales materials that really sell, how to set up your office—in short, all the tricks of the trade.
204 pp, $14.95

Creative Containers to Make and Decorate
by Madeleine Brehaut
Here's a guide to turning the very useful into the very beautiful: Step-by-step instructions for creating more than 40 interesting and unusual containers perfect for holding everything from floral arrangements to precious keepsakes.

128 pp, color throughout, 81/2 x 11, $19.95

New Ways with Polymer Clay
The Next Generation of Projects and Techniques
by Kris Richards
Explores a multitude of possibilities for conditioning, shaping, curing, and mixing colors of polymer clay. Ten projects, ranging in complexity from beginner to advanced, let you practice these techniques and have fun at the same time.
112 pp, color throughout, 81/4 x 107/8, $19.95

Coiled Pottery
Traditional and Contemporary Ways, Revised Edition
by Betty Blandino
In this popular book, author Betty Blandino surveys historical examples of coiled pottery and describes the methods of contemporary and ethnic potters who build in this way. The new edition features 16 pages of color photos as well as greatly expanded sections on contemporary artists and their decorative techniques, and on

contemporary handbuilding in general.
112 pp + 16 color pp, 71/2 x 91/8, $22.95

Fantastic Finishes
Paint Effects and Decorative Finishes for Over 30 Projects
by Nancy Snellen
In stunning color photos and clear, thorough step-by-step instructions, Fantastic Finishes presents an inspiring array of projects that incorporate the latest products and techniques.
128 pp, color throughout, 81/2 x 11, $19.95

Design for Survival
This video workshop presented by one of the nation's best-selling craft jewelers, Thomas Mann, will help you find your way through the complicated process of pricing craftwork for the marketplace. A "must" for beginners and established professional artists.
Thomas Mann, 1810 Magazine St., New Orleans LA 70130, 518.581.2111
www.thomasmann.com

PROFESSIONAL SERVICES

American Council for the Arts/ACA
1285 Avenue of the Americas
New York NY 10019
212.245.4510

American Federation of Arts
41 E. 65th St.
New York NY 10021
212.988.7700

Anne Childress, Copywriter Editor
5107 Wetheredsville Rd.
Baltimore MD 21207
410.448.3676

Artists Rights Society
Darla Decker
65 Bleecker St.
New York NY 10012
212.420.9160

Arts and Crafts Business Solutions
Guy McDonald
2804 Bishop Gate Dr.
Raleigh NC 27613
800.873.1192

Arts, Inc.
315 W. Ninth St. #201
Los Angeles CA 90015
213.627.9276

Bob Barrett, Photographer
323 Springtown
New Paltz NY 12561
914.255.8599

Business Volunteers for the Arts
410 Eighth St. N.W., #600
Washington DC 20004
202.638.2406

1200 One Union Sq.
600 University Ave.
Seattle WA 98101-3186
206.389.7272

25 W. 45th St.
New York NY 10036
212.819.9287

Charles Geser, Accountant
305 W. Chesapeake Ave.
Towson MD 21204
410.821.6300

Designing Wright
Debi Wright
1186 Queen Ln., #3
West Chester PA 19382
610.738.9253

Dynamic Focus Photography
1179 Tasman Dr.
Sunnyvale CA 94089
800.299.2515

Jerry Anthony Photography
3952 Shattuck Ave.
Columbus OH 43220
614.451.5207

Modern Postcard
6354 Corte Del Abeto
Carlsbad CA 92009
800.959.8365

Paper Chase Post Card Printing
7176 Sunset Blvd.
Los Angeles CA 90046
800.367.2737

Ralph Gabriner Photography
30 Madeline Pkwy.
Yonkers NY 10705
914.376.0175

Sally Ann Photography
Box 259543
Madison WI 53725-9543
608.273.9613

Steve Meltzer Photography
2927 Pinecrest St.
Sarasota FL 34329
941.924.8381

US Press
1628A James P. Rodgers Dr.
Valdosta GA 31601
800.227.7377

CRAFT SUPPLIES

A A Clouet
369 W. Fountain St.
Providence RI 02903
401.272.4100

A & C Distributors
P.O. Box 70228
San Diego CA 92167
800.995.9946

ALPEL Publishing
P.O. Box 203
Chambly Quebec
CANADA J3L 4B3
514.658.6205

ARA Imports
P.O. Box 41054
Brecksville OH 44141
216.838.1372

ART Art Studio Clay Company
1555 Louise Ave.
Elk Grove Village IL 60007
847.593.6060

AVL Looms
601 Orange St.
Chico CA 95921
800.626.9615

CRAFT SUPPLIES

Abbott Designs
Gary Abbott
P.O. Box 1311
Roswell GA 30077
770.594.0561

Across the Anvil Farrier Supply
112 E. Main St.
Azle TX 76020
817.444.1783

Aim Kilns Manufacturing
350 S.W. Wake Robin Ave.
Corvallis OR 97333
800.647.1624

Aleta's Rock Shop
1515 Plainfield Ave. N.E.
Grand Rapids MI 49505
616.363.5394

Alpha Faceting Supply, Inc.
P.O. Box 2133
Bremerton WA 98310
360.377.5629

Alpine Casting Company
3122 Karen Pl.
Colorado Springs CO 80907
800.365.2278

Amazon Drygoods
Davenport, IA
800.798.7979

American Art Clay Company
4717 W. 16th St.
Indianapolis IN 46222
317.244.6871

Anchor Tool & Supply
326 W. Westfield Ave.
Roselle Park, NJ 07928
908.245.7888

Anvil Brand Tool Company
P.O. Box 198
Lexington IL 61753
309.365.8270

Aquarius Studios
85 Ferell Rd.
Elmwood TN 38560
615.897.2695

Arizona Gems & Minerals
22025 N. Black Canyon Hwy.
Phoenix AZ 85027
602.780.4903

Australian Opal Imports
3170 Tillicum Rd., P.O. Box 44208
Victoria British Columbia
CANADA V9A 7H7
604.652.5553

Axner Pottery Supply
P.O. Box 1984
Guiedo FL 32765
800.843.7057

B & B Products, Inc.
18700 N. 107th Ave., #13
Sun City AZ 85373
602.933.2962

B & J Rock Shop
14744 Manchester Rd.
Ballwin MO 63011
314.394.4567

BFB Sales Ltd.
6535 Millcreek Dr., #8
Misissauga Ontario
CANADA L5N2M2
905.858.7888

Bamboula
27 W. 20th St.
New York NY 10011
212.675.2714

The Basket Works
77 Mellor Ave.
Baltimore MD 21228
410.747.8300

Beadbox, Inc.
10135 E. Via Linda, #C116
Scottsdale AZ 85258
800.232.3269

Beck's Warp 'N Weave
2815 34th St.
Lubbock TX 79410
800.658.6698

Bill Gangi Multisensory Arts
P.O. Box 64141
Tucson AZ 85728
602.577.7574

Bluebird Gemstones
P.O. Box 12284
Portland OR 97212
503.281.4101

Bombay Bazaar
P.O. Box 770727
Lakewood OH 44107
216.521.6548

Bonny Doon Engineering, Inc.
250 Tassett Ct.
Santa Cruz CA 95060
408.423.1023

Boothe Lights
P.O. Box 9
Clarkdale AZ 86324
520.634.2825

Bourget Brothers
1636 11th St.
Santa Monica CA 90404
310.450.6556

Bullseye Glass Company
3722 S.E. 21st Ave.
Portland OR 97202

Burda Patterns
P.O. Box 670628
Marietta GA 30066
800.241.6887

By Diane
1126 Ivon Ave.
Endicott NY 13760
607.754.0391

C&F Wholesale Ceramics
3241 E. 11th Ave.
Hialeah FL 33013
305.835.8200

CKE Publications
2840 Black Lake Blvd., #E
Olympia WA 98512
800.428.7402

Canyon Records & Indian Arts
4143 N. 16th St
Phoenix AZ 85016
602.266.4823

The Cargo Hold
P.O. Box 239
Charleston SC 29402
803.722.1377

Castlegate Farm
424 Kingwood Locktown Rd.
Flemington NJ 08822
908.996.6152

Centaur Forge
P.O. Box 340A
Burlington WI 53105
414.763.9175

**Ceramics Supply of New York
and New Jersey**
7 Rt. 46 W.
Lodi NJ 07644
201.340.3005

Claymaker
1240 N. 13th St.
San Jose CA 95112
408.295.3352

Cobun Creek Farm
Rt. 10, P.O. Box 15
Morgantown WV 26505
304.292.1907

Columbus Clay Company
1049 W. Fifth Ave.
Columbus OH 43212
614.294.1114

Connecticut Cane and Reed Company
P.O. Box 762
Manchester CT 06045
860.646.6586

Cotton Clouds Mail Order Yarns
5176 S. 14th Ave.
Safford AZ 85546
520.428.7000

Crystal Galleries
1036 N Citrus Ave.
Covina CA 91722
818.915.6553

Crystal Palace Yarns
3006 San Pablo Ave.
Berkeley CA 94702
510.548.9988

David H. Fell & Company, Inc.
6009 Bandini Blvd.
City of Commerce CA 90040
213.722.9992

CRAFT SUPPLIES

Decart, Inc.
P.O. Box 309
Morrisville VT 05661
800.232.3352

Designs on You
Barbara Wright
11 Elm Ave.
Newport News VA 23601
804.591.2169

Dharma Trading Company
P.O. Box 150916
San Rafael CA 94915
800.542.5227

Diamond Pacific Tool Corporation
2620 W. Main St.
Barstow CA 92311
619.255.1030

Discount Agate House
3401 N. Dodge Blvd.
Tucson AZ 85716
602.323.0781

Donna Sayers Fabulous Furs
700 Madison Ave.
Covington KY 41011
606.291.3300

Dragonfly Software
10 Crestwood Dr.
San Rafael CA 94901
415.455.9911

E.B. Fitler & Company
RD 2, Box 176-B
Milton DE 19968
302.684.1893

Eastern Art Glass
P.O. Box 341
Wyckoff NJ 07481
201.847.0001

Eastern Smelting & Refining Corporation
37-39 Bubier St.
Lynn MA 01901
617.599.9000

Elaine Martin Canopy Company
P.O. Box 261
Highwood IL 60040
847.945.9445

The Emerald Rainbow Pattern Club
P.O. Box 6241
Clearwater FL 34624
800.550.5746

Fashion Blueprints
2191 Blossom Valley Dr.
San Jose CA 95124
408.356.5291

Fry Metals Stained Glass Division
4100 Sixth Ave.
Altoona PA 16602
800.289.3797

Fusion Headquarters, Inc.
7402A S.W. Macadam Ave.
Portland OR 97219
503.245.7547

Gabriel's
P.O. Box 222
Unionville OH 44088
800.359.5166

Gallery Lighting
5214 Burleson Rd.
Austin TX 78744
800.256.7114

Ginger's Needleworks
P.O. Box 92047
Lafayette LA 70509
318.232.7847

The Glass Library
64 Woodstock Dr.
Newtown PA 18940
800.786.8720

GlassWear Studios
1197 Sherry Way
Livermore CA 94550
510.443.9139

Glastar Corporation
20721 Marilla St.
Chatsworth CA 91311
818.341.0301

Globe Union International, Inc.
1237 American Pkwy.
Richardson TX 75081
214.669.8181

Graphiko
P.O. Box 872
Osprey FL 34229
941.966.1864

Great Copy Patterns
P.O. Box 085329
Racine WI 53408
414.632.2660

Grobet-Vigor USA
750 Washington Ave.
Carlstadt NJ 07072
800.847.4188

Hauser & Miller
10950 Lin-Valle Dr.
St Louis MO 63123
800.462.7447

Heaven & Earth
RD 1, Box 25
Marshfield VT 05658
800.348.5155

Hong Kong Lapidaries, Inc.
2801 N. University Dr.
Coral Spring FL 33065
954.755.8777

Industrial Metals & Surplus, Inc.
240 N. Highland Ave.
Atlanta GA 30307
404.577.5005

JHB International
1955 S. Quince St.
Denver CO 80231
303.751.8100

JS Ritter Jewelers Supply
118 Preble St.
Portland ME 04101
800.962.1468

John Henry Florist Supply Company
5800 W. Grand River
Lansing MI 48906
800.788.0517

John McGuire Basket Supplies
398 S. Main St.
Geneva NY 14456
315.781.1251

Ken Quilt Manufacturing Company
113 Pattie St.
Wichita KS 67211
316.262.3438

Lamp Base Specialties
P.O. Box 171
Worth IL 60482
708.361.1199

Larry Paul Casting, Inc.
740 Sansom St., #410
Philadelphia PA 19106
215.928.1644

Loew-Cornell, Inc.
563 Chestnut Ave.
Teaneck NJ 07666
201.836.7070

Lois Ericson Design & Sew Patterns
P.O. Box 5222
Salem OR 97304

Mary Wales Loomis
1487 Parrott Dr.
San Mateo CA 94402-3633
415.345.8012

Maurice Goldman & Sons, Inc.
22 W. 48th St.
New York NY 10036
212.575.9555

McNeil Woodworks, Inc.
118 Garfield
Argonia KS 67004
316.435.6908

Microstamp Corporation
2770 E. Walnut St.
Pasadena CA 91107
818.793.9489

Minnesota Lapidary Supply Corporation
2825 Dupont Ave. S.
Minneapolis MN 55408
612.872.7211

NC Tool Company
6566 Hunt Rd AR
Pleasant Garden NC 27313
919.674.5654

Paragon Industries, Inc.
2011 S. Town East Blvd.
Mesquite TX 75149
214.288.7557

CRAFT SUPPLIES

The Paul Wissmach Glass Company, Inc.
P.O. Box 228
Paden City WV 26159
304.337.2253

Platina Casting Service
2 W. 47th St., #602
New York NY 10036
800.410.7257

Plum Gully and Accent Glass Company
330 Green Rd.
Manchester CT 06040
860.646.4920

Plymouth Reed & Cane Supply
1200 W. Ann Arbor Rd.
Plymouth MI 48170
313.455.2150

Pop Shop
RR 2, Box 1524
New Dam Rd.
Sanford ME 04073
207.324.5946

Precious Metals West, Fine Gold
608 S. Hill St., #407
Los Angeles CA 90014
213.689.4872

Quabbin Valley Woodworking
120 Federal St.
Belchertown MA 04073
413.323.0233

Quilting Books Unlimited
1911 W. Wilson
Batavia IL 60510
708.406.0237

Reactive Metals Studio, Inc.
P.O. Box 890
Clarkdale AZ 86324
602.634.3434

Rio Grande Display and Packaging
7500 Bluewater Rd., NW
Albuquerque NM 87121
800.637.8303

Rio Grande Tools & Equipment
4516 Anaheim Ave. N.E.
Albuquerque NM 87113
800.545.6566

Robert Bentley Gemstones
34 W. 46th St.
New York NY 10036
212.302.4846

Ross Metals
54 W. 47th St.
New York NY 10036
212.869.1407

SAF T POCKETS
822 N.W. Murray Blvd., #163
Portland OR 97229

Saral Paper Corporation
322 W. 57th St., #30T
New York NY 10019
212.247.0460

Schlaifer's Enameling Supplies
1012 Fair Oaks Ave., #170
South Pasadena CA 91030
800.525.5959

Sierra Stained Glass Studios, Inc.
416 15th St.
Modesto CA 95354
209.524.2310

Skycap
37 W. 19th St.
New York NY 10011
800.243.9227

Source One Lamp Bases
7600 Metcalf
Overland Park KS 66204
800.473.4527

St. Peter Woolen Mill
101 W. Broadway
St Peter MN 56082
507.931.3734

Stan Brown Arts & Crafts
13435 N.E. Whitaker Way
Portland OR 97230
800.547.5531

Stenciled Garden
53 Market Pl.
Stratford Ontario
CANADA N5A 1A4

Stockade Wood & Craft Supply
650 Woodlawn Rd. W., Unit 5C
Ontario
CANADA N1K 1B8
519.763.1050

Swest, Inc.
11090 N. Stemmons Freeway
P.O. Box 59389
Dallas TX 75229
800.527.5057

T B Hagstoz & Son, Inc.
709 Sansom St.
Philadelphia PA 19106
800.922.1006

The Thread Bare Pattern Company
P.O. Box 1484
Havelock NC 28532
919.447.4081

The Thrifty Needle
3233 Amber St.
Philadelphia PA 19134
800.324.9927

Tim Roark Imports
190 10th St. N.E.
Atlanta GA 30309
404.872.8937

Unique Glass Colors
Drawer 20
Logansport LA 71049
318.697.4401

Valee Studios Publications
P.O. Box 971
Mi Wuk Village CA 95346

Venture Tape Corporation
30 Commerce Rd.
Rockland MA 02370
617.331.5900

Vitrographics Publications
223 N. Guadalupe, #254
Santa Fe NM 87501
505.471.3850

Walrus Publications
587 Sargent Ave.
Winnipeg Manitoba
CANADA R3B 1W6
204.783.1117

Western Trading Post
32 Broadway
Denver CO 80209
303.777.7750

Whittemore Durgin
P.O. Box 2065NP
Hanover MA 02339
800.225.0380

Winona Trading Post
P.O. Box 324
Santa Fe NM 87504
505.988.4811